10

Steps
to Be a
Successful

Manager

Lisa Haneberg

2nd Edition

ATD Press is an internationally renowned source of insightful and practical information on
talent development, training, and professional development.

The sections describing the Bridges Model in step 9 are adapted from Haneberg, L. 2005.
Organization Development Basics. Alexandria, VA: ASTD Press, 58-60.

ATD Press
1640 King Street
Alexandria, VA 22314 USA

Ordering information: Books published by ATD Press can be purchased by visiting ATD's
website at www.td.org/books or by calling 800.628.2783 or 703.683.8100.

Library of Congress Control Number: 2019933794

ISBN-10: 1-949036-20-0
ISBN-13: 978-1-949036-20-6
e-ISBN: 978-1-949036-21-3

ATD Press Editorial Staff
Director: Kristine Luecker
Manager: Melissa Jones
Community of Practice Manager, Management: Ryan Changcoco
Developmental Editor: Kathryn Stafford
Text and Cover Design: Darrin Raaum
Printed by P.A. Hutchison Company, Mayfield, PA

|CONTENTS

Introduction

Management is the engine that drives our corporations. It ensures—or prevents—the daily completion of work and overall strategic implementation. This may sound very *things* oriented, but make no mistake; management is a people-driven job. Our organizations need managers who bring individuals and teams together such that they do their best work in the service of company goals. It's tough to be a great manager, but it's also fascinating, enriching, meaningful, and fun. And never boring when done well! Unfortunately, some managers struggle to succeed because they let barriers like these get in their way:

- They become a victim of circumstances. Managers are needed to improve the organization and its results, but corporate dysfunction or immaturity can seem overwhelming. It is important to own your role in making things better and to resist becoming part of the problem.
- They confuse the need to manage with the need to control. Some managers think that their job is to control people and operations. Control is a myth; you can't and should not try to control people. The manager's job is to ensure that people and processes are doing their very best work toward achieving the goals of the enterprise. To do this, managers must connect to and relate with people and enliven their motivation. Actions that attempt to control people move results in the opposite direction. Great management is focused, service oriented, and relationship driven.
- They let management become maintenance. It is the manager's responsibility to make something happen that would not have happened without them. Management should never turn into maintenance. If you are doing the same things every day and

spending most of your time maintaining your piece of the business, you are not actively managing. It's easy to fall into the trap of getting comfortable with success, but managers need to resist this urge and ensure that they continue to drive performance forward.

- They fail to tune up and realign. Management A produces Results A. If you want Results B, you cannot get there using Management A. Great managers periodically tune and align their practices and approaches to produce desired results. Corporate strategies, initiatives, and goals frequently change, requiring managers to change too.

Do you struggle with any of these barriers or others? Please don't get discouraged; nearly every manager I've met has, at some point in their career, been challenged by the cruddy bits of management. The good news is that you can reduce these and other daily pain points by consistently applying best practices for management like the ones I share in this book. You have the opportunity to make a significant impact on the business and your team members' lives. You'll need to blast through organizational politics and dysfunction. But that's why you're here! Embrace the challenge and triumph over management barriers. Make this the best job you will ever have.

Management and Leadership

Before I get into the specifics of the 10 steps, I want to address a common question: What's the difference between management and leadership? My perspective on this may differ from what you've heard before or read in books about leadership. First, I don't believe that management and leadership are different positions or jobs. Many companies distinguish managers and leaders based on their pecking order in the organization. That seems like nonsense to me. We see and experience leadership at all levels of the organization. Some people believe that leadership is something you do when you move beyond management— that leadership is a set of higher-level tasks and that it takes more skill to be a leader than it does to be a manager. This belief does not make sense either. In fact, people with all ranges of education and sophistication and at all organization levels can and do demonstrate leadership.

So let's draw the distinction. Management is a set of methods and practices—a regimen—that enables us to run a business or a piece of the business. It's a job. Leadership is not a job; it's the way we do the job.

Imagine four peer managers sitting in a meeting together discussing the progress of a major project. The discussion itself could be considered part of management—it's part of the process. Having update meetings about major initiatives is a management task. Let's say that one of those managers, you, demonstrates courage and initiates a frank discussion about concerns that the others are too chicken to bring up. At your prompting, the discussion addresses important issues that need to be defined and resolved. During that display of courage—in that moment while the four of you were managing—you demonstrated leadership.

We ought to be managers all the time and show leadership when it's needed. If you are an operations manager, you ought to be a great operations manager all the time and demonstrate leadership when the situation calls for it. The same is true at all levels of the organization. Frontline workers ought to be great frontline workers all the time and lead when necessary.

The 10 steps offered in this book fall into the category of good management practices. Along the way, I'll share examples of where and when leadership—the way you approach your work and relationships—will help you improve momentum and connectedness. To be most successful in a management job, you'll also demonstrate leadership.

What's New in the Second Edition? Alignment With the ACCEL Model

In 2015 and 2016, the Association for Talent Development (ATD) conducted survey-based research to determine the crucial skills for managerial success. They then outlined the top five skills—accountability, collaboration, communication, engagement, and listening and assessing—in the report *ACCEL: The Skills That Make a Winning Manager.*

I've been managing people, observing great and not-so-great managers, and writing about management for three decades. That's a long time! I was thrilled when I reviewed the ACCEL model because these five skills cut to the core of what's needed to manage people to bring out their best, engaged performance. These capabilities show up—or don't—in nearly every workplace encounter with predictable results. As I wrote in the opening paragraph of this introduction, management is a people-driven job and the skills highlighted in ACCEL are decidedly social.

When the ATD Press editors and I started talking about doing this second edition of *10 Steps to Be a Successful Manager,* we agreed that we should highlight the ACCEL model and align the book's content to support your development of these five important skills.

This edition is organized a bit differently from the original, and I've added new content that I think you're going to like a lot. That said, you won't see "Step 3: Accountability," or other chapter headings that match the ACCEL skill names, and here's why: The ACCEL model offers a road map for the skills or capabilities that managers need to succeed. The 10 Steps books, on the other hand, offer actionable best practices or techniques that managers should use to succeed. In other words Said another way, practicing the techniques suggested in this book will help you develop the ACCEL model skills.

As I've noted, these skills are fundamental to great management, and therefore they will support your efforts in many ways. The table on the next page details how the best practices presented in each chapter support your development of the ACCEL model skills.

Notice that several skills are cultivated in each step. This is natural and expected, especially when addressing people-oriented capabilities like listening, communicating, and working with others. We apply these skills in many ways and situations. And here's the good news: The time you spend building these five fundamental management skills will serve you well because they impact nearly every aspect of your job.

Chapter/Step	Builds				
	Accountability	Collaboration	Communication	Engagement	Listening and Assessing
Step 1. Know Your Business	X		X		X
Step 2. Work Well With Others		X	X	X	X
Step 3. Define and Model Excellence	X	X	X		
Step 4. Hire for Fit and Onboard for Success	X			X	X
Step 5. Use Pull Versus Push Motivation		X		X	X
Step 6. Reinforce and Reward the Nonnegotiables	X		X		X
Step 7. Bring Out the Best in Others		X		X	X
Step 8. Plan, Measure, and Adjust	X	X			X
Step 9. Manage Change and Transition			X		X
Step 10. Build a Career, Leave a Legacy	X	X			

Target Audience

This book is for managers at all levels and with varying years of experience. Whether you are a new manager or a seasoned pro, you need to tune and align your management skills to make sure your hard work is producing optimal results. If you're a more experienced manager, you can use the "Your Turn" section at the end of each chapter to refresh your daily regimens. As a new manager, you'll want to follow the recommendations in a more deliberate and methodical way. Be sure to use the provided worksheets, tables, figures, examples, and pointers to help you get the most from the book's recommendations. Those elements will help you envision the technique, and they offer suggestions for applying the best practices to your work.

Sequence of the Steps

I've intentionally put each of the steps in *10 Steps to Be a Successful Manager* in a particular order. Whether you are a new or experienced manager, this book will work well if you follow the steps in the order I recommend. Some steps can be completed in a single meeting or planning session; other steps will take months to accomplish. You can begin working on the next step before the previous one is complete.

That said, remember that management isn't like changing a light bulb, with specific actions that must come one before the other. Management is a multifaceted position, not a single process. If you find it beneficial to skip around the book, that's fine—with this one recommendation: Do steps 1 and 2 in order and before moving on to the rest. The work of steps 1 and 2 is important and most often overlooked. Underperforming managers almost always need to retune and align those two steps.

Structure of This Book

10 Steps to Be a Successful Manager will help you establish or realign your management practices and regimens for improved results and satisfaction. Each step in this book describes one area of action you need to develop to create a robust and healthy management practice.

Here is a summary of each step:

Step 1: Know Your Business. Not all management jobs are the same, and it's important that you understand your role as defined by your manager, employees, and peers. To manage well, you need to know what home-run performance will look like for the portion of the business you manage—in the next month, six months, the next year, and beyond. Great managers know what is working well and where their managerial regimen needs more attention.

Step 2: Work Well With Others. Management is a social act. It occurs in conversation and within the context of several organizational teams. Managers who are excellent team players and leaders will have more opportunities to make a difference and to influence others. Make sure you are a terrific partner.

Step 3: Define and Model Excellence. Your team members want to succeed, but can only do so if they clearly understand what excellence looks like. How do you define and share expectations, including teaming standards? In addition to what you say, your day-to-day actions define expectations and excellence.

Step 4: Hire for Fit and Onboard for Success. You have a chance to improve the strength and effectiveness of your team each time you fill an open position. The decision to hire affects you and your team for years, so it is important that you hire for fit. Learn how to determine job, culture, and team fit and make hiring and promotion decisions consistent with your definition of excellence and performance expectations. Ensure that your onboarding program enhances job embeddedness (connections to the job, team, and company) for better employee retention.

Step 5: Use Pull Versus Push Motivation. Engagement is a choice; managers cannot require that employees be engaged. Creating a work environment that has more pull for team members is one way managers can enhance engagement and satisfaction. Learn how to create workplaces with more pull, and how focusing on engagement does not need to compete with or contradict efforts to improve accountability.

Step 6: Reinforce and Reward the Nonnegotiables. Managers, by definition, manage performance. Explore the fundamental building blocks of a highly accountable workplace and learn ways to effectively communicate feedback and requests, including how to handle difficult or uncomfortable conversations.

Step 7: Bring Out the Best in Others. An engaged and focused team needs less supervision and more coaching. When you hire and promote talented people, you are able to direct your time and energy toward proactive and meaningful endeavors. Learn the questions you should ask your team and employees to build job satisfaction and support their career development goals.

Step 8: Plan, Measure, and Adjust. Work planning is essential to tame your mile-long need-to-do and want-to-do lists. There are ways you can ensure your team is focused on the right tasks at the right time. Explore when to kill projects and shift people's energy to more important or fruitful initiatives. Learn ways to ensure you and your team know what's working and where additional attention or a change might be needed to ensure deliverables are met. To help team members complete their work on time and well, relish your barrier obliterator role. Managers exist to facilitate the forward movement of work. Identifying and getting rid of barriers is a great use of time that will improve results and morale.

Step 9: Manage Change and Transition. Change is inevitable, but how people respond to change is a choice. It's important that your department be nimble in the face of change. There are many things managers can do to promote smoother transitions when changes occur. It's also important to be ready for change. Learn ways to improve your and your team's agility to improve alignment and results.

Step 10: Build a Career, Leave a Legacy. Why are you a manager and what difference do you hope to make? Knowing "what's in it for you" is important and helpful. Great managers build teams and improve organizations. Learn how to hone your managerial regimen so that you leave a legacy consistent with your goals.

Review the 10 steps once a quarter or as your business goals change to ensure that your hard work yields the greatest benefit and job satisfaction.

Being a manager can be a blast because, as the engine of the organization, you can set the tone and pace for success. What could be more fun and rewarding than that?

Step 1
Know Your Business

Overview

- Clarify behavior expectations.
- Define operational excellence.
- Measure your managerial effectiveness.

In the introduction, I asserted that management is the engine that drives organizational results. Let that idea sink in for a moment, because it's heavy. As a manager, you are an engine—you power forward movement. Your company has handed you a piece of the business, and your job is to help that department, division, location, or operating group manifest its goals. Your prime directive is to make good things happen. Whoa! Cool! Yikes! This is a significant burden and privilege, and I encourage you to feel the weight of it. Your work is important.

POINTER

When expectations are not comprehensive and clear, it is very difficult to make good choices about how to spend your limited time.

So how should you go about approaching your role as the engine for a part of the business? How do you make sure your efforts yield the best results? This book answers these questions beginning with step 1, which will help you see the big picture of your management assignment.

Clarify Behavior Expectations

Let's stipulate that many well-meaning, hard-working, talented managers stink at communicating and clarifying expectations. Your boss, your boss's boss, my former bosses, all of us. Why? Because people are busy, because their boss hasn't done it, because they've never thought about expectations beyond basic job duties. But here's the thing. Even if your well-meaning, hard-working, talented, and otherwise awesome boss stinks at sharing their behavioral expectations, you need to seek clarity.

You need to seek clarity.

You want to know—really know—the behavioral expectations that your manager, peers, and team members have of you. How can you be an effective engine for a piece of the business if you don't? How can you make good things happen if you don't know how "good management" is defined? Sadly, most managers don't know how they're supposed to act. Especially not to the depth and degree that they need in order to be optimally successful. So that's why we will start our exploration of management here.

Behavior expectation conversations often occur only after something goes wrong and in conjunction with performance counseling. Perhaps you ruffled feathers, had a public meltdown, failed to be accountable, chased staff members away, or treated someone unfairly. These corrective conversations are important but not what we are talking about in this managerial step.

You need to know much more and before concerns arise. You want to know the type of work environment you should be cultivating. You want to know your part in leading and enabling change. You want to know your manager's expectations regarding creativity and innovation. You want to know the organization's professionalism standards in detail because there are always differences from company to company. You want to know what your manager expects in terms of employee engagement, accountability, and development. You want to know what your peers want from you as a partner and colleague. You want to know the type of manager your team members hope you'll be. And you want to know so much more.

OK, Lisa, I get it. I want to know about the many types of behavior expectations. How do I do this?

Answer: You ask. You ask your manager, peers, and employees specific questions that yield specific and helpful answers. Tool 1-1 offers a meaty list of questions that you can use to clarify behavior expectations. I recommend setting aside 60 minutes per meeting for the first round of conversations, and then allowing 20 to 30 minutes to update expectations. Try doing the following:

- Have a one-on-one conversation with your manager.
- Gather several of your peers together and ask them questions. (This makes for a very interesting conversation because while you'll clarify the behavior expectations they have of you, you'll also get to reinforce your expectations of them.)
- Ask your employees, first in a group meeting and then one-on-one as part of your regular conversations. If team members seem uncomfortable sharing their ideas in front of you, break them into smaller groups and then allow them to report out their group's input.

This might sound like a lot of meetings, but you only have to do it occasionally. Use Tool 1-1 as a starting point for the conversation and add your own questions. And here's an idea: Some of these questions can be tried at home! So while you are at it, use portions of this tool to generate a great discussion with your spouse or significant other. OK, maybe you don't want to know that. . . .

TOOL 1-1

QUESTIONS TO DETERMINE BEHAVIOR EXPECTATIONS

Topic Area	Questions to Ask
Basic Job Function	• How do you define quality of work? • What are your expectations regarding deadlines and communication of work status? • What does being prepared mean? • How will you measure my success?
Decision Making	• What is your expectation of me regarding making and communicating decisions? • What types of decisions would you like me to make and when do you want to weigh in?

Topic Area	Questions to Ask
Work Environment	• Describe the work environment you expect me to build and reinforce. • In what ways would you like to see the company's culture change and what role do you believe I should play in creating that transformation? • Is there anything about the department's current culture that you think ought to change or improve?
Creativity and Innovation	• How important is creativity and innovation this year and what are your expectations of me regarding this? • In what areas would you most like me and my group to generate new ideas and improve results?
Team Development and Productivity	• Describe how a well-functioning team looks and feels. • What expectations do you have regarding team development and productivity? • What are your expectations regarding how I will manage and correct poor performance? • How much time do you think I ought to spend coaching others?
Communication	• What does effective communication look like? • What are your expectations of me regarding communication? • What are your expectations of me regarding attending and conducting meetings?
Growth and Development	• Everyone needs to continue to grow. In what two ways would you most like to see me develop over the next year?
Results Orientation	• What do you think it means to be results oriented? • How will you measure my success beyond operational metrics?
Partnership	• Describe great partnership and collaboration. • With whom should I partner the most? • In what ways would you like to see partnership and collaboration improve?
Ethics and Role Modeling	• I know I'm expected to be a role model, but what's most important in this regard? • What does it mean to represent the company well? • What are your expectations for how managers conduct themselves?

STEP 1

The questions listed in Tool 1-1 are great, right? I realize it might seem a bit overwhelming, but you can select and adjust the questions based on who you're meeting with and where you need clarity. It's worth the effort to do this—I promise. Clarify behavior expectations annually, or twice a year if your job or focus changes. In addition, don't miss the chance to calibrate your understanding of behavior expectations throughout the year. Things change and memories fail. Take advantage of opportunities to clarify individual expectations when discussing specific projects, goals, or new departmental challenges. Take a look at Tool 1-2 for some common behavior expectations for managers.

POINTER

Clarify behavior expectations annually, or twice a year if your job or focus changes.

TOOL 1-2
COMMON BEHAVIOR EXPECTATIONS FOR MANAGERS

Some aspects of management are common across industries and for all levels of responsibility. Here are several behavior expectations that apply to all managers. Consider sharing this list with your manager and discussing specific examples of desired behaviors for those that apply to your role. Record feedback you receive and action planning to ensure your development stays on track.

Managers Should...	What This Means	Feedback and Action Planning
Be highly accountable.	This includes clarifying performance standards, providing feedback, measuring progress, rewarding achievement, and addressing poor performance. It is also important to hold oneself to a high standard and to humbly admit setbacks.	

TOOL 1-2. COMMON BEHAVIOR EXPECTATIONS FOR MANAGERS (CONT.)

Managers Should...	What This Means	Feedback and Action Planning
Think creatively, be proactive, and take initiative to improve their team's performance.	They should seek to improve some aspect of the work or workplace every day. It is not a manager's job to maintain or oversee what would happen on its own.	
Manage based on metrics.	This includes creating, communicating, and managing based on meaningful measures of performance, results, and productivity. They should involve peers and team members in the process of establishing and monitoring key metrics.	
Build and maintain productive work relationships.	With every meeting and every conversation in which they participate, managers have the opportunity to either add to or detract from the quality of the relationship. They should seek to repair relationship issues and be deliberate about spending quality time with peers, team members, and key stakeholders, including their manager. Operating in isolation will not yield success.	
Cultivate flexible and nimble teams.	They should have their finger on the pulse of the company and know when changes in approach make sense. Managers should not be overly comfortable with the status quo and should actively support employees through change-related angst and ambiguity.	
Be responsive to other people's ideas and concerns.	This includes being coachable when offered feedback and seeking input and feedback to enable continuous learning.	

Managers Should...	What This Means	Feedback and Action Planning
Know when to lead—and do so.	This may demand courage and might mean taking risks. Moments of leadership inspire and align people and the organization.	
Help employees do their best work in the service of the organization's goals.	They should create work environments that enable and encourage employee engagement and that inspire intrinsic motivation.	
Be outstanding behavioral role models every day and in all workplace situations.	They need to represent the best of what they seek in others and practice effective stress-management techniques to constructively manage times of frustration or difficulty.	

Are you high or on drugs? I imagine this might be the question that comes to mind after you collect and consider everyone's behavior expectations. You can't stuff 200 pounds into a 100-pound bag (but we try, don't we?). And remember, this initial inquiry does not include project-specific operational goals or work products. Even so, this first pass often yields a significant amount of input and too many daunting behavior expectations to count.

So, here's one more expectation. It's your job to negotiate behavior expectations so that you can be successful. Sometimes you don't have the time, resources, or skills to achieve it all and sometimes you need to get a better understanding of what the expectations mean. Here is a common expectation:

> Managers must represent the needs of both the company and their employees. They're the lens that helps both senior management see things from the frontline employee's perspective and frontline employees see through the senior managers' eyes.

Sounds good, but what does this mean and look like in action? Who knows? It's important to discuss and understand. When I was a manager, I did a behavior expectations tune-up quarterly and then made sure that actions and words were clarified and aligned. Doing that was important to me because I wanted to stay focused on what most mattered.

Clarifying behavior expectations will help you understand what others hope you will do as you manage your piece of the business. This is a critical part of knowing your business and setting yourself up for success. It is also important that you know how great work is defined for the operational aspects of your work.

Define Operational Excellence

Let's take our understanding of job expectations to the next level—to the hitting it out of the park level. Good performance is getting it done, but excellence is hitting a grand-slam home run, as in baseball. The grand-slam home run (which yields the maximum of four runs) makes the most out of the team's efforts and has an added benefit of creating a feeling of success—elation!—throughout the organization.

I like using this metaphor for excellent operational results because everything we do ought to have a positive and additive effect on our teams, peers, and the organization. If you are going to do something, make it a grand slam!

Sounds nice, but let's put this metaphor into action. Start by listing all your key projects, initiatives, and core business processes. If you are an accounting manager, for example, purchase orders might be a core process. For each item, define your current metrics or performance measures. Next, meet with your manager. Review what you've recorded so far and then make the following request:

> I know that there's more to these goals than these basic measures, and I want to make sure that my team and I are focused on what's most important. I'd love to brainstorm with

you what a grand-slam home run would look like for each one of these operational goals that includes productivity, process, behavior, and culture considerations. I have an example of what I'm talking about here.

How does that sound? Here's the example you can share with your manager, which deals with a project to implement the new accounting system within budget by August 1. A grand-slam home run might be to:

- Complete the implementation by July 15, before the busy season.
- Involve the accounting team such that ownership and acceptance is high.
- Implement the project while improving accountant computer skills so they can better use the new system's features.
- Develop robust contingency plans to cover any potential project setbacks.
- Reduce the costs spent on the project by harnessing the creativity of the group to find the best way to transition to the new system.

There's getting a project done and then there's managing a project such that many other aspects of the work are improved as well. That's excellence. As a driven and talented manager, you want to know how your manager defines excellence. Actually, you'll need to know because you need to be able to define excellence for your team, as we'll see in step 3.

You might be thinking that talking about excellence will set you up for failure because the boss will then expect nothing but grand slams from you and your team. It's true that openly discussing grand slams does change things—for you and your boss—but this is a good thing. Your conversations will become more useful, important, and motivational. And

POINTER

Define and strive for the grand-slam home run to have the deepest and broadest positive impact on the organization.

you'll develop a stronger business relationship as you go beyond dinking around along the surface of performance conversations. My goal with this step is to help set you and your team up to succeed at a level you've not previously imagined. If you don't identify what a grand slam looks like, what do you think the chances will be that you'll know to focus on each of these desired outcomes? You might know or guess some of them, but not all. We get what we focus on.

If you include the behavioral expectations discussion at your next one-on-one with your manager, discuss operational excellence at the one after that. Or you can book one longer meeting to do both if that works better for you and your manager. You can call it *planning for success* or something like that. Example 1-1 shows you how you might set up the information for the grand-slam discussion with your manager.

What a cool and helpful process! Once you have typed up your operational goals with grand-slam home run performance indicators, share it again with your manager to confirm that you interpreted their input correctly and get agreement on your top priorities. Hold the spreadsheet in your hand and breathe a sigh of relief—many managers haven't a clue what they are supposed to do, but now you do! It feels great to understand, in depth, the results that you should produce for the organization. And it's satisfying to know how your manager defines excellence. I love clarity, don't you? Use your spreadsheet as a discussion guide during regular one-on-ones with your manager and for the weekly planning you do with peers and your team and employees (you do both of those things, right?).

POINTER

As a driven and talented manager, you want to know how your manager defines excellence.

One caveat about all this clarity, though—things change. You'll want to update your chart monthly or as needed. It is important that it always contains the current version of grand-slam home runs and what's most important.

Example 1-1
Excellence: Grand-Slam Home Run Goals

Operational Goals	Current Metrics	Grand-Slam Performance	Progress and Next Actions
Implement new accounting system	August 1 Budget $XXX Training for all users	Complete implementation by July 15, before the busy season. Involve the accounting team so ownership and acceptance is high. Implement the project while improving accountant computer skills (so they can better use the new system's features). Develop robust contingency plans to cover any potential project setbacks. Find a way to do this and reduce project costs—harness the group's creativity to find the best way to transition to the new system.	Timing on target. Expand team involvement. Contingency plan draft by end of month. Identify opportunities for cost reduction at next update (involve team).
Project B			
Core Process A			
Core Process B			
Initiative A			

Using this process to define extraordinary results will put some additional pressure on you (and therefore your team) to perform at a higher level—but it's all good. Would you like to know that you need to climb to the summit of Mount Rainier or would you prefer to remain oblivious to that expectation and fool around in the foothills all year long? If you know the summit is your target, you'll prepare, train, and approach the mountain ready for the long journey. Here's an important point—whether you have the grand-slam conversation with your manager or not, the grand slam is already in their mind. Your manager wants excellence. If you don't take the time to define grand slams, you'll miss out on an opportunity to align with their hopes for you and your department.

POINTER

Your manager expects the grand slam whether or not you define what that looks like.

Once you clarify behavior expectations and operational excellence, you'll want to ensure that your managerial practices support your success. Time is precious! But how do you know if what you're doing will lead to the results you seek?

Measure Your Managerial Effectiveness

You manager just stopped by your workspace. After some pleasant banter, she mentions that she'd like you to update her on how things are going at your next one-on-one. Specifically, she's interested in your managerial efforts and how she can best support you. The one-on-one is in two days. Do you know what you're going to say? Or will you be burning the midnight oil for the next two days to prepare?

You might be thinking that your boss does not sound like this example and would never make a request or offer like this. So, this is a moot point. You don't need to prepare for a meeting that will never happen! Right?

Wrong.

While your manager might not specifically ask for it, they want to know how things are going for you—as a manager—and how they can best help. And you want to know, because you want your time and effort to yield the best outcomes.

At any given moment, you should be able to self-assess your performance relative to behavior expectations and grand-slam goals. I'll admit that measuring managerial behaviors is less straightforward than keeping your operational goals chart up to date. But here's the thing: Management is visible—what you do is observable and can be measured. Here's an example using one of the behavior expectations for all managers that I suggested earlier in the chapter:

> Managers should be responsive to other people's ideas and concerns.

Are you delivering on this expectation? Here are a few ideas for how you might self-assess your performance:

- Assess your meeting agendas and determine the percentage of time you spend seeking and listening to concerns, ideas, and input from others.
- Record and acknowledge ideas from others that you have implemented.
- Make it a habit to send thank you emails or notes to others when they offer ideas. Reflect on how often you thank others each month.
- Measure your follow-through of concerns from the time each concern is communicated until it has been addressed or resolved.
- Ask employees and peers for feedback on your responsiveness to their concerns and ideas.

Now, I know what you're thinking. You're worried that if you measure your performance against every expectation, you'll not have any time to *manage*. This is a valid concern, and doubly so if you're the type of person drawn to data analytics and more likely to go down the measurement rabbit hole. I don't want you to become an absentee manager because you are in your office check-sheeting your meeting minutes.

But here's the bottom line. Select and use metrics that will illuminate how you're doing on your top priorities. Be choosey. If you want to be a stronger role model, focus on metrics that help you understand your impact on others. If creating a more collaborative work environment is an important behavioral goal, then make sure you have good metrics that tell you how you're doing.

POINTER

Measurement takes time and energy—make sure you are measuring meaningful indicators of your success.

Be careful, however, that you measure the right indicators. For example, if you want to increase collaboration, don't measure the number of meetings you schedule and hold (this is almost always a terrible measure); instead, assess what's happening when people work together in meetings and other business discussions.

Step 1 is called Know Your Business because *management is your business*. You are the engine hired to power a part of the organization. To be a successful manager, you need to know what's expected of you and how your boss and other key stakeholders define excellence.

Building ACCEL Skills

The management techniques we've explored in step 1 will help you build the following ACCEL skills:

- **Accountability.** Step 1 emphasizes personal accountability by helping you develop skills to define what you need to do to be successful. When you understand what you need to accomplish and own, it will be easier for you to create an accountability culture for your team.
- **Communication.** If you practice clarifying expectations and excellence, you will build important communication skills that help you improve focus, manage team performance, and negotiate with peers.
- **Listening and assessing.** Step 1 focuses a lot on having conversations that will help you understand the piece of the business that you've been asked to manage. You will find

that the more you practice these conversations, the better you will be able to listen deeply and assess the meaning of what you hear.

Your Turn

It can be a bit intimidating if you've never asked questions about expectations or grand-slam home runs before. To get started, try these methods:

- Find a mentor with whom you can discuss and practice your approach. If you verbalize the questions ahead of time, you can tweak your list and get more comfortable with them.
- Ask a peer to practice with you and offer to do the same for them. That way, you will both benefit and be more prepared.
- Prepare talking points that help provide context about why you are asking these questions. It is important that your boss knows that you want to know their expectations because you are interested in succeeding, not because you wish to complain about them.

The Next Step

Knowing your business provides an important foundation from which you can manage. Once you understand what—in the broadest sense—you are being asked to do, you can explore the best ways to make it all happen. Remember, managers make thing happen! In step 2, you'll learn about the most important and profound managerial characteristics you should cultivate to be a successful manager.

Step 2
Work Well With Others

Overview

- Learn how management is a social act.
- Show that you care.
- Build strong relationships.
- Be a great partner.
- See how dysfunction reverberates.

This book is about managerial success, but let's talk about failure for a moment. I've been writing about management for a long time, and I've held many managerial roles. I've sat across the table from managers who were having very bad days because they were being counseled or terminated. And I've coached managers who were struggling. I personally know of the circumstances involving dozens—if not hundreds—of managers who lost their jobs, and here's what I've noticed. Managers don't fail because they lack technical skills. The most common reason that managers struggle or fail is that they don't work well with others. Hint: This is also why clarifying behavior expectations was the first thing we explored in step 1. It's not just what we do that matters, but how we do it, and how what we do affects others.

Let's define a few terms before we explore step 2 further. Managers work within organizations, and things get done because individuals and their teams know what to do and they do it. Most of

POINTER

The most common reason managers struggle or fail is that they don't work well with others.

what gets done in an organization happens because many people come together to make it happen. This may seem like an obvious statement, but think about its ramifications. If organizational success requires groups of people who are making things happen, then working well with others is a fundamental requirement for success. This is even more true for managers who, by the nature of their work, need to partner and influence several levels of the organization every day.

Working well with others means that you're a pleasure to work with. People like working with you because you're positive, pleasant, and responsive. Working well with others also means that you do your part and are dependable. When you say you'll have it done tomorrow, you have it done tomorrow. It's about integrity. It's about relationships. It's about teaming.

But please don't misunderstand. Although I'm suggesting that being a pleasure to work with is critical for your success, I'm not saying that you should lack determination or deliberateness or hesitate to take initiative. Quite the opposite actually, since your initiative can also help you work well with others.

If you're one of those managers who says, "I am who I am, and they can take me or leave me," however, take heed. Maybe you're naturally pessimistic or grouchy, or are unpleasant before your third cup of coffee, or work with your door closed to avoid interacting with people. Remember the observation I shared in the opening paragraph to this chapter—the most common reason managers fail is that they don't work well with others. How well you work with others may be more important than your individual contributions to your organization.

POINTER

How well you work with others may be more important than your individual contributions to your organization.

This is some serious stuff, I know. And no pressure, but the answer to the question, "Do I have to be likable?" is *yes!* You have to be likable, responsive, and a great partner.

Management Is a Social Act

Do you have a whiteboard, chalkboard, or corkboard in your office? If so, put up this statement right now: *Management is a social act.*

Management is a social act; it occurs in conversations of all types—discussions, emails, texts, and gestures. Conversations are your currency for getting things done. As a manager, you are an engine for organizational results, and conversations are your fuel for making things happen. You can't manage in isolation.

Management is a social act and to be successful, you need to be a great conversationalist. But that doesn't mean chitchat or shooting the breeze or giving a TED talk. While those are all good things to do when appropriate, they're not what I'm referring to when I suggest conversations are your engine fuel.

You also don't need to be an extrovert to succeed. I'm an introvert, and I know many introverts who are amazing managers. I don't care if you are the life of the party. Personally, I hate parties!

So what do I mean, then? Let's break down the key words:

- **social**—relating to a society, a group of people who are together for a common purpose
- **act**—deliberate action, observable action, doing something
- **conversation**—messages sent and received between two or more people.

Being a great conversationalist in the workplace means that you help enable, facilitate, or initiate connections between people that help them move work forward. When you internalize and accept that management is a social act, it will change how you approach your work. This is a good thing.

Here's a true story. I taught 25 sessions of a two-day management class to 500 participants who worked for a major metropolitan city. After one of the classes, a manager walked up to me and shared that the distinction, *management is a social act,* had been helpful. She managed a supply chain function and had been promoted from

POINTER

Management is a social act; it occurs in conversations.

a line-level role in the same group. She was very comfortable with data, Excel spreadsheets, and reports. And while she loved the supply chain function, her love of the work was creating a challenge. She was spending very little time in conversation and therefore, very little time managing. She decided to write "management is a social act" on the top of her whiteboard, which she faced when sitting at her desk. She felt that seeing it several times each day would serve as a reminder to get up and out of her office and into conversation. To spend more time managing. It was an epiphany for her, and one that she felt would change how she spent her precious time.

We all have mile-long to-do lists and lots of things to get done that don't involve *management*. And some of us enjoy the satisfaction of checking items off our list. Maybe—likely—we love the technical aspects of our function and find these tasks satisfying or more measurable. But make no mistake, doing those things is not management. That's why I suggest that you write *management is a social act* somewhere in your workspace to help you remember to connect with people. Together, you move work forward.

Check out Tool 2-1, which lists several cues you can use to ensure that you are spending time in catalytic conversations (catalytic meaning making things easier or better).

Review this list at the beginning of each workday and add your own common cues. Make decisions about how you spend your time based on the results. This simple practice will improve your managerial effectiveness and help you work better with others. I promise! But there's more to step 2, so let's keep discovering.

TOOL 2-1
WORKPLACE CUES THAT A CONVERSATION MIGHT BE NEEDED

Cue	Consider
Work tasks are late.	Seek to learn about barriers employees are facing. Discuss delays in an open and supportive manner. Discuss opportunities to improve processes with peers. Work with employees to make adjustments so they can focus on top priorities.

Cue	Consider
You feel out of the loop.	Spend more time rounding (regular informal check-ins, sharing of information). Ask for and appreciate updates. Go to lunch with a peer. Ask open-ended questions during your next one-on-one. Share information with others (doing so encourages similar behavior).
Employees email a lot of questions.	Seek to understand if there is a need for training. Invite peers or others to share information with your team and address questions. Take time during staff meetings to share information and answer questions.
Few people talk in staff meetings.	Ask interesting, open-ended questions and positively reinforce participation. Let employees know your questions before the meeting so they can prepare. Make discussion a significant part of the agenda (versus rushing through many updates). Break into groups of two or three employees who report out their input. Assign team members to lead discussion topics on a rotating basis.
A peer misinterprets your email or text.	Talk to your peers more often (they'll be less likely to misinterpret). Have more in-person conversations, especially when the topic is important, complicated, or emotionally charged. Share regret, apologize for not being clear and clarify intent.
You hear concerns that are not shared in meetings.	Encourage those who express a concern to share it in a forum that can address it. Listen and ask questions that help you understand people's concerns–often the initial complaint is a symptom, not the problem. Connect those with concerns to people who can address them. Resist perpetuating rumors. Share information that helps reduce incorrect assumptions.
There seems to be a lack of ownership or interest in goals.	Share goals with employees. Encourage an open discussion of goals and alternatives. Share back-story and context–the "why" for new projects and initiatives (as appropriate). Invite project leaders and subject matter experts to share information with your team. Listen and respond to concerns.

Show That You Care

I have a feeling that some of you are rolling your eyes at the title for this section. I get it; "show that you care" sounds a bit like "floss your teeth" territory, but please stick with me for a moment. Remember the opening observation of step 2: Managers who fail often do so because they don't work well with others.

A number of these failures occur because peers and employees don't like to work with the manager. I recall one situation where a team of about 18 employees marched down to the VP of human resources' office and declared they did not want to work for their manager. I'm going to call her Sally. Can you imagine being Sally? What about being an employee on Sally's team? How long had the employees been unhappy before they decided to complain? The answer is many months. This is a true story and not all that uncommon, albeit it is less common that employees complain en masse to HR.

I was assigned to figure out what was going on and recommend how to resolve it. This included getting to know the manager. Sally had worked for the company for nearly 15 years and had been promoted from within several times because of her technical knowledge and attention to detail, eventually reaching the role of manager. After spending that long with the company, what are the odds were that she did not care? Very low. In fact, she cared deeply, she was just terrible at showing it. Case in point, she:

- barked at her employees
- spent each morning reviewing errors and quality problems
- rarely walked around the department unless she needed something
- did not present herself as cheerful or positive
- never asked how people were doing or how she could help.

Why did Sally act this way? Partly because she was too busy with to-do list tasks to pay attention to her employees, partly because she was socially awkward and had not practiced showing care (her husband and kids likely got similar treatment), partly because she did not understand that management is a social act, and partly because she was scared and intimidated. I remember that when the investigation was complete and I reviewed the findings with her, Sally asked me point blank, "Are you telling me that I need to be liked as a manager to be a manager?" *Yep, Sally, that's exactly what I'm telling you and much more.*

Let me contrast this story of struggle with an example of success:

I recently spent an afternoon with a business colleague and friend who is also a manager who "works well with others" better than anyone I know. When he's around others they know they have his full attention and consideration, and they do (it's sincere; not an act). He notices people and situations and takes the initiative to be helpful and caring, more so than most of us.

I've always known this about my friend but was vividly reminded during our walk that afternoon. Those we passed received a smile and hello. When we saw a baby bottle someone had dropped, he picked it up and put it on the cement wall so the owner could find it and no one would trip over it. When we came upon a couple taking pictures of each other, he asked if he could take their picture together and then had some fun with them to make sure they got a great shot. He interacted with people on the street, in shops, and in the restaurant where we had lunch in ways that made each person smile and brighten.

You might be thinking that I am silly for calling this out because these human acts are quite normal—or they should be. None of these moments were significant or extraordinary. I've done things like this and I'm sure you have, too. But here's the distinction. He showed care in every moment. He was aware of others, noticed others, and proactively cared for others; and he did so while remaining fully engaged in our conversation.

And this translates to his work, too. My friend is someone people love working for. He brings out the best in others with his attention and interest. We can and should do this, too. You don't need to take a training class or embody a particular behavioral style. We can relate to others by:

- choosing to be a powerful and positive influence
- taking the time and attention to notice others
- being gracious, kind, friendly, and helpful.

But you don't need to add these expectations to your performance review or create a management competency called "caring." Just try being more demonstrably caring and see what happens. Manage from a basis of positive care for others and you will find that your days, weeks, and years are more fruitful and that your good vibe spreads.

You've likely heard this saying: *If a tree falls in a forest but no one is there to hear it, does it make a sound?* Well, I wonder if caring really exists if no one experiences our affection and goodwill. Most people, especially managers, care deeply. Why especially managers? Because management is a tough gig and one that we choose and take because we want to help others. However, even though most of us care—remember, Sally cared—we don't always demonstrate that care such that others know and feel our positive intent. When it comes to your impact on others, perhaps it counts only when observed, received, and understood by them. That puts a lot more pressure on us, but it's appropriate pressure.

Thankfully, it's not hard or burdensome to make caring for others a more deliberate part of our daily regimen. Tiny actions—smiles, pictures, gestures of help—add up to make a big impression. Try including some of these into your daily routine:

- greeting staff and co-workers warmly
- remembering important days or milestones
- offering support
- removing a persistent barrier that's standing in the way of or slowing an employee's or peer's progress
- showing interest
- expressing encouragement
- acknowledging strengths and accomplishments
- being available
- informal rounding in person or virtually for the purpose of checking in (not just asking for something).

POINTER

When it comes to your impact on others, perhaps it only counts when they observe, receive, and understand it.

But the benefit of being more well-liked should not be the reason that we choose to live a more generous (of ourselves) life. In other words, the caring must be genuine. This is not a management technique that you should track on a check sheet, although you might put ticklers on your calendar that prompt you to round or MBWA (manage by wandering around) for a few minutes. The friend

I mentioned earlier does not wake up in the morning and plot how he will win people over. He simply cares about people and takes the initiative to show it.

Build Strong Relationships

Working well with others supports your ability to influence them. For managers, influence is critical to moving work forward and making things happen. Influence comes from others being willing to listen to you. Are you being heard? Are your ideas being considered? Are your concerns taken seriously? Are you included in discussions? Management is a social act, and influence is what happens when your conversations make a positive difference.

Building strong workplace relationships will help you improve influence. Peers, team members, bosses, and others are more likely to consider and be influenced by your input or suggestions if you've built a relationship with them. In the workplace, a relationship is a bond between you and another person you work with. Having a relationship requires you to know something about the other person and for them to know something about you. Your relationship needs some common interest or goal or circumstance. Why? Relationships exists when we *relate*.

Relationships help you manage. You've heard about the danger of first impressions and snap judgments, right? They're often wrong. Sometimes way wrong! When we first see, hear, or observe someone we make up stories about what we're seeing to make sense of it. But we don't know the real story until we get to know that person.

Building relationships is doubly important for managers. You need to take action using good information based on accurate assumptions, and to do that you have to go beyond first impressions and surface-level acquaintances and get to know people for who they really are, what they're trying to do, and why they're doing it. I know that you have some great relationships at work; we all do. But many of us are lopsided when it comes to building relationships. We:

- have a few friends that we spend more time with than others

- let relationships just happen, or not
- hang out with people who are like us, in our same function, or with similar interests.

These natural selection methods are fine when developing friendships, but they're inadequate when it comes to determining the workplace relationships that you'll need to succeed. Working well with others means all others, especially those we work with regularly, such as team members, peers, bosses, key stakeholders, mentors, and support functions (for example, finance, human resources, or the supply chain).

Busy managers often don't spend the time or effort needed to build and maintain relationships at work. And I get that. You're already feeling like your to-do list is too long and growing. Working well with others is a priority, however, and building relationships is a core part of this step. Take a few moments to complete Worksheet 2-1.

Building relationships is not just about meeting with people, of course. But one-on-one discussions are often a great place to start. The getting to know you meeting—where you each share a bit about each other, your goals and priorities, and ways that your work overlaps, collides, or differs—is still one of the best ways to kickstart this process. Building and maintaining productive relationships enables you to create an effective partnership, which is the next part of working well with others that we'll explore.

Be a Great Partner

Partnership is one of those words like *communication* and *collaboration* that gets tossed around a lot but often isn't clarified to the point of being actionable. For managers, partnership requires mutual trust, shared purpose, shared ownership, critical thinking, shared success and failure, and effective inclusion and communication. That may sound like a lot, but simply boils down to having a foundation in place such that you do great work together. That's our job: to do great work with others and to be an amazing partner so that our managerial engine drives the forward movement of goals, initiatives, projects, and people development.

POINTER

That's our job: to do great work with others.

WORKSHEET 2-1
RELATIONSHIP BUILDING PLANNING WORKSHEET

Consider the relationship building strategies for each co-worker grouping. Reflect upon what you're currently doing and record the action steps you think might be beneficial. Use this worksheet to request and schedule meetings or other actions. Prioritize the actions in co-worker grouping 1, as these are the most important relationships to cultivate.

Grouping 1

Co-Workers	Relationship Building Strategies	Action Plan
• Direct reports • Upstream peers • Downstream peers • Your manager • Mentor or coach • HR partner	• Greet them warmly when you see them • Meet monthly • Have informal coffee chats • Hold brief check-ins every one to two days • Provide regular updates by email or when rounding • Include work and priority planning and development planning when setting goals • Key group of people to "show you care"	

Grouping 2

Co-Workers	Relationship Building Strategies	Action Plan
• Other reports • Peers you'll partner with during the next six months • Key support partners	• Greet them warmly when you see them • Meet with them quarterly • Have informal coffee chats if projects and priorities warrant • Include them in your targeted goal setting • Provide proactive updates	

Grouping 3

Co-Workers	Relationship Building Strategies	Action Plan
• Other stakeholders • Your boss's boss • People with jobs you aspire to	• Greet them warmly when you see them • Meet with them once or twice a year	

Who should you be partnering with? Everyone will have a different list of key partners, but most managers focus on peers, fellow project team members, and support group personnel (for example, finance and HR).

What does partnership look like in action? It's a beautiful thing when talented professionals work well together as partners. They co-create, co-lead, co-own, and co-control. Let's explore what partnership looks like in more detail. Tool 2-2 lists several techniques you can use to develop and demonstrate partnership.

TOOL 2-2
PARTNERSHIP TECHNIQUES

Practice	Summary
Spend time together	Management is a social act. The more time management team members spend working with one another, the easier and more natural the partnering process will feel. In addition, peers who get together often are more comfortable asking for input, help, and participation than those who see each other only at staff meetings. And it all counts—meetings, informal conversations, events, and other social gatherings.
Don't try to control peers	If you demonstrate a persistent need to control situations, people, or conversations, it will undermine effective collaboration with your peer group. Partnering is a give-and-take process; no one gets to play boss all the time. Listen and watch for verbal and nonverbal cues that suggest other people are feeling pressured or pushed. Ask more open-ended questions and make fewer opinionated statements.
Resolve relationship problems	Unresolved conflicts affect the way people relate to one another. Take the initiative to resolve prior relationship issues to pave the way for better a partnership. The benefits of working through conflicts will make up for the initial discomfort of broaching the topic with the other person. If a peer doesn't seem willing to improve the relationship, you can do one of two things. First you might try a different approach. Can you look at the situation from their perspective? It may be that what you thought was the problem is not. Second, you are the only person you can control. Even if your peer is hanging onto a grudge, make sure that you continue to act and relate in a manner that is professional and collaborative.

Practice	Summary
Represent each other well	In addition to communicating well with one another, it is important for peers to communicate well on one another's behalf. Represent your peers' interests and needs in staff meetings, brainstorming sessions, and informal conversations when they are not present. You may need to defend a peer's budget choices or represent their opinions and concerns. Great partners do this even when they don't agree with their peers' point of view. When representing your peers in a positive light, you communicate that respect and care for colleagues is a key value.
Never badmouth	Never badmouth peers in front of others—it will burn bridges that you'll likely need in the future. Always speak respectfully. Managers who talk about other people behind their backs look bad themselves because it's immature, unprofessional, and destructive. This is not to say that disagreements with peers should be ignored. It's healthy to push back and challenge each other in a professional way. You need to deal with differences of opinion or disagreements directly and productively with the person involved.
Own your problems and challenges	Don't pass the buck. Few situations can put a damper on a partnership faster than being hung out to dry by a peer. If you have a complaint about how another manager is handling a situation, speak to that manager directly before bringing it to your boss or the team.
Be humble	Success comes from collaboration, and all players should share credit. Managers who ensure that everyone feels like part of the success will enjoy positive momentum going into the next project for initiative. "Be humble" also means showing gratitude for your relationships with peers. Managing is a privilege and humble managers know this.
Know their needs	You'll find it easier to be a good partner if you understand the needs and motivations of your fellow managers. This allows you to anticipate their needs, warn them of emerging problems, and share helpful ideas with peers. What are their goals, interests, and priorities? What unique skills and talents do they bring to the company? What can you learn from them? What are their hot buttons? What do you expect from them, and what do they expect from you? How is your work co-dependent?

STEP 2

How are you doing? Are there practices in Tool 2-2 that you should add to your managerial regimen? Keep them in mind as we continue learning how to work well with others.

Dysfunction Reverberates

It's a regular part of my management training courses to discuss the downsides of generating dysfunction. In fact, participants cheer and give me high-fives when they see we're going to be talking about dysfunction. Kidding! I'm more likely to see eyerolls and disappointment. But once we get into it, we always end up having lively and important discussions.

And here's the most important distinction. Dysfunction reverberates; it echoes and expands. Like the water droplet that causes ripples covering the entire puddle. There's always some dysfunction in an organization, but as managers we should aim to reduce dysfunction where we can and not add to it. When people fail to work well together, many are affected. Here's a typical sequence of events that will occur after something happens within a team meeting to cause tension or conflict:

1. Conversations are less fruitful, and members move toward the meeting room door instead of digging deep to clarify or resolve the issue.

2. Upstream and downstream internal customers are affected because those differences spill into team member discussions and affect their quality of work.

3. Those around the team feel the pain, as the stress and tension are shared like hot Hollywood gossip.

4. Bosses and bosses' bosses get involved. Sometimes they help; sometimes they perpetuate or magnify the tension.

5. Even those with no direct involvement hear about the issue and take sides. And even if they don't take sides, they'll certainly feel tension about the tension.

6. Something that started small causes a major mojo malfunction (that's the technical term for bringing down the vibe in the workplace).

Now imagine that the team members are managers instead of individual contributors. The reverberation of their dysfunction becomes much wider, and "goes viral" very quickly. Managers cannot expect their employees to be any more committed and passionate about the business than they demonstrate. The same adage goes for teaming. As a manager, you cannot expect your staff to work well together if you and your peer team don't seem to care enough to role model the desired behaviors.

Dysfunction is often a symptom of inadequate relationship building. This is a topic I feel strongly about, and I'm going to assert something that you might find brash or bold. Management team dysfunction is irresponsible and immature, and I cannot fathom what is going on in someone's head that rationalizes why it is OK to waste their time and their peers' time because (for example) they don't like someone's style. You don't like someone's style? Are you kidding me? Managers should hold themselves to a higher standard and have similarly high standards for the team members who report to them. Clashes in style or approach or opinions should never get in the way of working well together. Never. It is well worth the time you need to invest to build strong peer relationships and well worth biting your tongue on occasion (or putting your ego temporarily aside).

I've observed peers who generate dysfunction, while others partner well in spite of their differences. The distinction between these two groups is often that the latter took the time and energy to build strong relationships. This takes some work, of course, and you might not learn what's amazing about your peers until the third or fourth time you partner with them. We are all amazingly talented and terrifically flawed, and the more we can get to know one another the more we can appreciate what's amazing

POINTER

Dysfunction reverberates—it echoes and expands.

and support each other's growth. And perhaps, just perhaps, we can make amazing things happen together.

We've covered a lot in this chapter. Your success has more to do with your ability to work well with others than almost anything else.

Of all the steps shared in this book, this one could have the most profound effect on your ability to manage well.

THE SANDBOX THEORY OF MANAGERIAL SUCCESS AND FAILURE

I am doing a training session tomorrow and one of the topics I am discussing is sandbox issues. Here's the "cliff notes" version.

Assertion: Sandbox issues are at the core of most managerial setbacks and problems.

Sandbox Defined: A real or imagined territory.

Sandbox Issue Defined: Problems (drama, mostly) that occur when people try to climb into our sandbox or when we try to climb into other people's sandboxes.

Reality: There is no sandbox—we are imagining it all. Like a mirage for someone thirsty for an ego stroke. This is an organization. Work and people are interdependent. We might have accountability, but we don't have territory. Other people have every right to hop into our imagined sandbox and muck about. If they aren't, it is likely because we are scaring them away and this is irresponsible.

Here's the bottom line. We need to get rid of the stories we tell ourselves about sandboxes. We need to invite people into our sandboxes (especially since they don't really exist), even when they do not yet possess the savvy to do that well. And we should build the skills to climb into other people's imagined sandboxes without causing drama.

Eventually, if we get good at this—especially if our peers do the same—we'll stop seeing sandboxes. That's right: No sandboxes, just one humongous beach.

Here's your challenge for today: What could you say to coach yourself into not feeling tense or irritated when others approach your sandbox, and what can you do to invite more people into your sandbox?

(This originally appeared in my Management Craft Blog, June 6, 2012.)

Building ACCEL Skills

The management techniques we've explored in step 2 will help you build the following ACCEL skills:

- **Collaboration:** Building relationships, showing that you care, and demonstrating partnership will support your efforts to collaborate more fully.
- **Communication:** We explored communication techniques and barriers in all five sections of this chapter. Effective communication is an essential part of working well with others.
- **Engagement:** While there might not be a direct or obvious connection between this step and employee engagement, the two are quite interdependent. Working well with others creates a positive and purposeful energy that will serve your efforts to increase employee engagement.
- **Listening and assessing:** To work well with others—to show care, build relationships, partner, and reduce dysfunction—you must listen well. As you practice the techniques presented in step 2, you will notice that you're spending more time listening and that the conversations you are having are more substantive.

Your Turn

Working well with others is a practice you'll hone and cultivate your entire career. Here are a few things you can do now to focus your development:

- Reflect on the five sections within this chapter. Review the tools, exercises, and sidebars. Jot down a short list of actions you think might benefit you most.
- Discuss the topic of working well with others with your manager and mentor or coach. Ask for feedback about your strengths and on which areas they believe your development should focus. Keep an open mind and be coachable. This

area of performance—our teaming behaviors—tends to feel more personal, so it could evoke an emotional response.

- For one week, focus on showing that you care. However, don't be over-the-top or creepy about it. Be visible, walk around more, and greet people with a kind word. See how you feel at the end of the week and adjust your plan for the following week.

- Notice how dysfunction starts and spreads. Think about changes—actions or behaviors—that could've prevented disagreements or miscommunications from creating dysfunction within your team. Use these observations to better manage the situations you face each day.

The Next Step

So far, we've focused on building an effective overall approach to *your* work. In the next step, you'll use what you've learned in steps 1 and 2 to better manage your team.

Step 3
Define and Model Excellence

Overview

- Define excellence.
- Set expectations for teaming.
- Communicate your vision of excellence.
- Act consistently with your definition of excellence.

We explored the concept of *excellence* a bit in step 1. It's a lofty word that we throw around a lot in training courses and books like this one. It's too bad that we don't talk more about excellence while we're at work—what does it look like on Tuesday at 2 p.m. or during the Friday morning huddle. Excellent performance, after all, is very, very good! A common reason why we don't see more excellent performance is that we don't talk about what it looks like and how we'd know it if we saw it in action.

I made the case for why you should talk about excellence in the form of grand-slam home run goals in step 1 so that you could be laser-focused on what most matters. In step 3, you will provide the same type of clarity for your team. Talking about excellence is powerful because conversations create reality. Your staff will make choices about what to do and how to do it based on their understanding of your expectations.

Here's a challenge for all managers: You should define and describe excellence and how it is brought to life. Simply saying "excellence is doing a great job" or "excellence is no mistakes" is a cop-out; it's not helpful.

Define Excellence

Imagine that your team is thriving and performing at the top of its game—grand-slams every day! Now look around and write down what you see. What are you most proud of? Describe how things work; how work flows through the department and between employees. How are people communicating? Describe a typical day-in-the-life—what's happening to you and your employees? What happens when problems arise? Is this a creative workplace? If yes, how so? What kind of innovation is happening? Describe how employees work with one another to implement projects. What does learning and relationship building look like in your world of excellence?

Put together a one-page description of excellence for your department and then add a paragraph or two for each unique position. It's fine (and would be awesome) to involve your team members in creating a vision of excellence, and your team members need to know how you define it. Check out Example 3-1 for an example. It's a real definition of excellence that I created with a client company for its management team (I've removed the company name and proprietary information).

This exercise will help you use scenario planning thinking, which Thomas Chermack, author of *Scenario Planning in Organizations: How to Create, Use, and Assess Scenarios,* defines as "a discipline for building alternative futures in which decisions can be played out for the purposes of changing thinking, improving decision making; fostering individual, team, and organizational learning; and improving performance." I recommend *Scenario Planning in Organizations* to all managers and shared more about Chermack's work in The *ASTD Management Development Handbook,* which I curated for ATD.

POINTER

Your team needs to know how you define excellent performance.

Example 3-1
Managerial Excellence at ABCo

You and your team are focused on what's most important, and you produce extraordinary results. People work at a brisk pace, but they do not feel burned out. Employees are clear about priorities and how their work ties to departmental and corporate goals.

Your work environment encourages team members to do their best work and execute well. They feel challenged and important. Communication is open, candid, and focused on the business. Although they know they are accountable for results, employees are driven by their intrinsic motivation to excel and accomplish.

You know time is a precious resource and you ensure that you and your team use it wisely. Meetings are called only when necessary, and they are well run. Conversations are lively, provocative, evocative, and focused. People are eager to participate in business dialogue and to contribute their ideas and concerns. You and your team have become excellent conversationalists. Even so, you do not bog people down with unnecessary meetings, emails, conference calls, or written material.

You know that saying "no" is just as important as saying "yes." You demonstrate focus and courage to make sure that your team does not get buried with projects or tasks that are nice to do but would not make it to the list of what's most important. You productively partner with your manager and peers to prioritize work that will best support the company's goals and reject projects that do not. Your focus helps you and your team produce results and serve your internal and external customers.

You have tuned your department to best serve the needs of your internal and external customers. You aggressively eliminate barriers to providing outstanding service, and you reengineer processes and practices that support your operations. You acknowledge the importance of serving internal customers such that external customers are better served and satisfied. You work proactively with peers to ensure that interdepartmental processes and practices are effective.

STEP 3

The only constant is change. You and your team are nimble; able to zig and zag to changing needs and conditions. You respond to emerging needs and do not hesitate to readjust tasks and work flow when needed. You help your team adjust and come to terms with change.

You know you are the face of ABCo and play an important role in helping the company grow and mature. You model excellence and are a pleasure to work with. You are regarded as trustworthy and reliable. Employees want to be a member of your team, and they know you will support their needs and goals. You take administrative responsibilities seriously and complete forms and reports on time. As an agent for the company, you make good judgments on its behalf and protect it from unacceptable risk.

This is what managerial excellence looks like, and we know that each of our managers can achieve this level of contribution. Some of you might need to question a few habits or learn new skills. The journey will be well worth it. Imagine what work will feel like when you reach managerial excellence. The impact you will have on the organization will be inspiring and significant in terms of tangible results. You will feel like you make a difference every day. Strong teams will stay together and do great work. ABCo will be a better, stronger, and more sought-after company—by prospective employees and customers.

What do you think? As a manager, does reading this description give you any ideas for how you can make a positive contribution every day? Your definition of excellence ought to be inspiring and challenging—you're going for excellence, after all, not mediocrity. You want to do knock-it-out-of-the park work. Once you've defined excellence, shout it out from the top of the building! Use Worksheet 3-1 to help create your vision of excellence for your function, employees, and team.

WORKSHEET 3-1
TEAM EXCELLENCE WORKSHEET

Describe excellence for each performance factor. Be specific.

Performance Factor	How Do You Define Excellence?
Key accomplishments, results	
Communication	
Collaboration	
Professionalism	
Creativity and innovation	
Project performance	
Meetings	
Problem identifying and solving	
Change and agility	
Reputation within the organization	
Teaming	

Set Expectations for Teaming

I'd like to explore one aspect of defining excellence a bit deeper—your expectations regarding teaming. I've seen managers struggle to share their behavioral standards for what it means to be a great team member. And many don't clarify even minimum expectations for teaming until there's a problem. That's too late and not enough, given its importance.

Teaming behaviors are an enormous asset when they are strong and an equally enormous problem when they are lacking. Here's a true story. I was talking with a manager who had a team that was struggling. Several team members were acting like bullies, and they had been seen yelling, swearing, and gossiping. In the same breath, this manager mentioned that his team members were good performers in terms of their job tasks.

> **POINTER**
>
> Teaming behaviors are an enormous asset when they are strong and an equally enormous problem when they are lacking.

Do you see the crux of the problem?

The manager viewed teaming as something other than a basic job duty.

Wrong! I suggested that he move teaming expectations into the category of basic job tasks—not something nice to have, but performance that is expected and required. *Work* is a team endeavor, and yelling at someone is a failing of a fundamental performance expectation.

Are teaming expectations held to the same level of importance and accountability as technical job tasks in your workplace? They should be. More teams fail to meet their goals due to teaming issues than they do because of poor technical skills. And if it's excellence that you seek, and you should, then it is important to define what excellent teaming looks like. Consider the following elements of teaming and describe how the workplace will look and feel if the team is excellent (this is a deeper, but narrower dive into the vision you articulated earlier in the chapter):

- How are team members interacting?
- How do they resolve conflicts?
- What are they sharing?
- How are they participating?
- What do they learn from one another?
- How do they welcome new members to the team?

You might also want to distinguish behaviors that are clearly not teaming excellence such as gossiping, negative demeanor, failure to participate, or poor collaboration.

Communicate Your Vision of Excellence

Let's start this section with tips for how *not* to communicate your definition of excellence. Don't share your vision for team excellence like it's the minimum expectation. Try not to describe excellent performance the way a drill sergeant would bark mess hall duties. Don't rely too heavily on check sheets or put excellence into SMART (specific, measurable, attainable, relevant, time-bound) goal terms.

Excellence is a vision. It's an aspirational and, hopefully, inspirational picture of what things are like when everything clicks and hums. Excellence is a story—not an assignment.

Here's how I share my vision of excellence with my team. First, I gather them together in a meeting room and schedule the meeting for one hour. I bring muffins if the meeting is in the morning and cookies in the afternoon. I tell them it's always good to understand where each team member is coming from regarding beliefs about how we can best do our work, and that I believe it's helpful for everyone to know how I define excellence. After sharing my vision of excellence in detail, I ask for reactions and questions, inviting people to share their thoughts about excellence. I show my gratitude for their input. I let them know that personally and as the manager of the team, I want to shoot for excellence and I hope they do too. I tell them they can depend on me giving honest and frequent feedback, and that I appreciate the energy and passion they pour into the work.

You should communicate your definition of excellence in a way that's consistent with your style, but make sure you're specific in describing your vision; describe excellence in a way that inspires your team; and invite input, reactions, and open conversation.

At the start of your regular staff and project team meetings, take five minutes to read and refresh the vision of excellence. When people bring up ideas, questions, and concerns, ask for alternatives that would best support excellence.

Act Consistently With Your Definition of Excellence

Your ability to communicate a vision of excellence and to improve performance can be hampered if your actions contradict it. Here are a couple examples of how you can inadvertently confuse your message and expectations:

- You say that you want to create an environment where productive and energetic conversations occur during meetings—but then put your team through the usual, and dreaded, go-around-the-table staff meetings.
- You say excellence means that everyone contributes ideas and has the opportunity to lead—but then bog your people down in routine tasks and offer no forum for sharing ideas.
- You say that teaming is important—but then you promote someone with strong technical experience who alienates others and is often uncooperative.

One of the most difficult aspects of management is the need to behave consistently with our goals, visions, and the behaviors you want to see in others. As managers, we don't get to be confusing. We need to think about what we're doing each day and ensure that it's in alignment with how we want to influence performance.

You've taken the time to define what excellence looks like. If you want excellence, make sure that your actions, practices, and habits support what you seek. Table 3-1 offers a few more common inconsistencies I've observed.

Think about the actions you took yesterday. How many of them support your vision of excellence? The more consistent your actions, the clearer your vision will become for all team members. Defining, communicating, and modeling a vision for excellence are powerful ways to ensure that your team is set up for success. It's tough to hit a target when you can see it, but it's nearly impossible when you can't.

It's also a great idea to bring steps 1 (know your business) and 3 (define and model team excellence) together now. Do you see how the products of these steps combine to help you plan and run your piece of the business? The efforts you make here also make great communication tools.

POINTER

Make sure your actions don't inadvertently contradict your definition of excellence.

Your team members want to succeed but can do so only if they clearly understand what excellence looks like. Give them the gift of clarity, and they will reward you with greater performance and focus.

TABLE 3-1
WHEN WHAT MANAGERS SAY IS EXCELLENCE DOESN'T
MATCH THEIR ACTIONS

What They Say	But What They Do
They value candor and diversity.	They become defensive when challenged or when people offer alternative ideas.
They want meetings to be productive and move work forward.	They facilitate ineffective meetings and book meetings that aren't viewed as a good use of time.
They value collaboration and teamwork.	They reward and reinforce only or primarily individual contributions.
They expect all employees to model the highest standards of professionalism.	They gossip and denigrate peer managers in front of team members.
They want the team to be change-resilient and agile.	They resist changes that make them personally uncomfortable or require a lot of work.
They want the team to be customer-focused and provide excellent internal and external service.	They neglect to collect or listen to customer feedback or measure the team's performance based on customer-centric metrics.
They want the team to think creatively and generate ideas for improvement.	They don't support team members who want to get together to share and discuss ideas.

STEP 3

Building ACCEL Skills

The management techniques we've explored in step 3, "Define and Model Excellence," will help you build the following ACCEL skills:

- **Accountability:** Accountability systems require that you start by clarifying expectations—many managers struggle with this. By practicing defining and communicating excellence, you will improve your skills in this area.
- **Collaboration:** Collaboration is easy until expectations clash or roles become unclear. Learning to define and communicate

excellence—especially with regard to teaming—enables you to better foster workplace collaboration.

- **Communication:** As a manager, communicating requests regarding performance—especially behavior—can be tough or scary. The skills we explored in this chapter will help you come across more clearly and directly with regard to performance expectations.

Your Turn

Here are a few ways you can practice defining excellence for your team:

- Read the sample definition of excellence I provided in this chapter. Then take a stab at articulating your vision of excellence. Ask your peers and team members for input and ideas.
- In one-on-one meetings with team members, make sure that each person understands how you'll evaluate excellence for their job. It's important to negotiate and calibrate your expectations. It is also helpful to ask what they expect of you and how they would define excellence for your role. Enlightening!
- Take the pressure off yourself for the first draft. Set the expectation that your definition of excellence will be a living and breathing document. Make changes and keep it updated.
- Use this same technique for project teams, peer groups (should be a collaborative process), and even your family.

The Next Step

Defining and communicating excellence helps you manage team performance. It also assists you when making hiring decisions. Step 4 explores how to use what you've defined in step 3 to better hire for fit.

Step 4

Hire for Fit and Onboard for Success

Overview

- Define job, culture, and team fit criteria.
- Interview deeply and well.
- Onboard well.

There are few things in this world that I know for sure, but this is one: Our ability to hire the right people for our job openings will significantly affect everything else we do as managers. Hiring right is critical. A strong team will give us the time and flexibility to focus on high-impact work. It's important to be very picky when hiring, and we don't want to settle for someone who's not the *right fit for the position*. Let me repeat these important words again—the right fit for the position (and organization). Your objective is not to find the person with the highest IQ or greatest number of years of experience; it's to find the right person for a particular job at a particular time.

One of the most effective ways to reduce the need for counseling or termination conversations is to hire the right people in the first place. Poor job fit is a common reason newer employees fail.

POINTER

Passionately communicate your definition of excellence, using specifics that enable people to form a mental picture of excellence in action.

The desire to fill open positions may tempt busy managers to accept marginal candidates, but that's never the best solution or the right thing to do. Never! Keep your job-fit standards and expectations high. The right person can infuse the team with positive energy and valuable skills.

Define Job, Culture, and Team Fit Criteria

How do I write this politely and with some level of political correctness? Oh, forget about it, I'll just type what I'm thinking—most job descriptions stink as recruiting tools. They stink for a few reasons; but mainly, many job descriptions don't describe the most important aspects of the job, and they rarely describe behavioral expectations fully enough. I'd encourage you to partner with the human resources team to ensure your job descriptions are relevant and useful, but I also want to make sure you know their limitations as a hiring tool.

Job descriptions generally don't address job fit, or the type of person you're seeking for the role. The bottom line? Writing a job description is not the same as defining criteria for job fit. I recommend that you create fit criteria for all open positions; at a minimum create them for all commonly recruited positions. When determining the criteria, you'll want to look at job fit, culture fit, and team fit. Here are some questions to ask to help you determine who will most likely succeed for an open position:

- What type of person will best be able to succeed, given:
  - work tasks
  - team dynamics
  - departmental work environment
  - corporate culture
- Think about those who are or have been successful doing this job. What skills or behaviors most contributed to their success?
- Over the next year, what changes or improvements will need to be made (for example, moving to a new computerized order process)?
- Given the relative strengths and weaknesses of the other team members, what type of person would best help the

team rise to the next level of performance? What skills and experiences does the team need?

- What type of person will best challenge me and help push our department forward?
- How does this role fit in terms of job progression with other roles?

Refer to your definition of team excellence from step 3 to help you define the hiring criteria for new team members. You want to hire employees who have the potential to model excellence, right?

I've done a lot of hiring and have coached managers on how to hire for fit. A common pitfall is overvaluing one aspect of a candidate's qualifications. Hiring someone with lots of experience can be awesome, for example, but only if the person is a good fit in other ways as well. Here's a statement I hope you'll internalize and remember.

STEP 4

Most people are not a fit for your open jobs.

This is not a bad thing; it's the way it ought to be. Think about five businesses in your home city. Most of them would not be a great fit for you—even within similar industries. For example, when I lived in Seattle there were two large coffee companies that competed for talent—Starbucks and Tully's. I often thought I'd like to work with Tully's, but not Starbucks. Why? I like a scrappy, entrepreneurial environment, and Tully's seemed to fit that more than Starbucks. Also, I thought Starbucks had gotten so big so fast that it might be harder to have an impact (like steering the *Titanic*).

What's the work environment that represents a fit for you? And what is your current work environment like? You'll need to hire with your current culture in mind (as well as your goals for how the culture should change) to select the best candidate. This is also the case when considering internal candidates— doubly so for promotions. If you don't take the time to define the criteria for job fit, you'll have no way to know how well each candidate matches up with what you're seeking.

POINTER

Most people are not a fit for your open jobs.

Once you've defined the job, culture, and team fit criteria, make sure that the essence of this information is included in job postings and ads. You want to attract the best candidates and provide enough information that will allow those who are not at all a fit to self-select out of the search. I know, some people will apply for the role even though they are not a fit for it, but others will opt out and this is a good thing. Fit is everything.

Interviewing Deeply and Well

We've arrived at a topic that is near and dear to my heart: interviewing. Think what you will, but interviewing is the best tool we have to hire for fit and it's often underutilized. Here's a question for you:

> Is a job interview a test or a conversation?

Think about how you conduct interviews. Do you shine a bright light in the eyes of hopeful candidates or subject them to verbal firing squads of five-on-one group interviews? Do you ask "gotcha" questions in the hopes that you'll trip up candidates so you can eliminate them from the applicant pool? If you do any of these things, you might be treating the interview process as a test. A job interview ought to be a conversation—a two-way discussion that lets you get to know the candidate, and vice versa.

I've noticed that some managers don't spend enough time interviewing candidates—whether on initial phone conversations or in-person interviews. Perhaps they're relying on their intuition or gut (wrong choice). Perhaps they believe anyone with technical experience should be given a shot (wrong again). Perhaps they're relying on interviews with others or pre-employment tests to give them the information they need to make a decision (wrong and wrong; although both are helpful and may be part of a good hiring process). Or perhaps they're just abdicating their responsibility to making good hiring decisions!

POINTER

A job interview isn't a test; it should be a conversation.

Those are strong words, I know, but they're true. I recommend that you spend as much time as you need to determine if the candidate is a fit for your open role. *And* plan time for the candidate to get to know you and ask you questions, because they need to determine if your role is a fit for them. You might need to interview some candidates more than once, and this is fine and normal. I know you are very busy, but you'll never regret the time if you hire the right person.

A quick word about group interviews, of which I'm not a fan. It's important that you recognize their use and limitations. They don't usually lead to a good hiring-for-fit conversation. Relationships are not built, and you're subjecting the candidate to stress, which might inhibit their ability to open up and share experiences. I once was interviewed by a group of 12 people, including the CEO and several members of his senior leadership team. As a facilitator, I was able to handle the conversation (but most candidates will not have that background). Did I really get to know any of them? No. Did they really get to know me? No. All they learned was that I could facilitate a conversation with 12 people. Peer interviews can be helpful to allow the candidate to meet the team and vice versa, but they should not be used as the primary interview from which a decision will be made.

Here are a few other recommendations for how to interview deeply and well, and find the candidate who's the best fit for your open position:

- Don't expect human resources to own the process of filling your position. Too many managers abdicate ownership of hiring, and that's a big mistake. Who needs to train this person? Who needs to manage this person? Who'll be responsible for ensuring this person is productive? On whose team will this person reside? You and yours. Personally, I would not ask HR to narrow the candidates to a list you ought to interview. There might be an unconventional rock star in the pile of résumés, and HR is more likely to screen based on job descriptions. Take the time to be very involved from the get-go. Nothing against HR; I've been a human resources manager myself. But they don't know your needs and team like you do, and they won't be managing the hire. It's in your best interest to get and stay involved.

- Use behavioral interviewing. Behavior-based questions tell you more about how candidates have approached their work and how they've responded to various situations. Past performance is the best predictor of future performance. Collaborate with your HR partner to cultivate a list of behavioral interview questions for your roles. Example 4-1 lists several behavioral interviewing questions I've used when talking to candidates for management positions.

- Use behavioral interview questions, but don't let them get in the way of having a great conversation about the job, company, and the candidate's qualifications (ask candidates only about information directly related to their qualifications for the job—no personal questions; work with HR for more specifics). Take time for conversation that's specific to experiences and interests. If you're not skilled in interviewing techniques, seek training or coaching. Competence at interviewing is necessary to make the right people decisions.

- When talking to each candidate, get to know their motivation for submitting an application. What do they want to get from the position? What work do they most enjoy? If you're hiring a manager, determine whether the candidate has a genuine interest in and capacity for management—management experience is not enough.

- Ask multiple people to interview each candidate—one-on-one. Yes, I know this will add to the overall time it takes to interview and choose between top candidates, but it's worth the investment. Make sure the interviewers know your criteria for fit. Have a group debriefing meeting to get feedback. If someone has a bad or really good feeling about a candidate, take that seriously and look into it further. Conduct a follow-up interview if needed.

- Give candidates lots of time to ask questions. It's important that they have an opportunity to get to know you and learn what they need to determine their level of interest. You can tell a lot about how a candidate thinks by the questions they ask. If there are no questions, that's a concern. If all the questions are about pay and benefits, that's a red flag too. I want to hire someone who's interested in the business and work—interested enough to have done some research and come to the interview prepared with several business-related queries.

POINTER

Although you are interviewing the candidate, they are also interviewing you.

- Share information with candidates. Tell them about your role and career, what you're like as a manager, the goals of the department, and about the team. Let them know a bit about the workplace culture and broadly about the team (for example, most have been with company for many years, very diverse, high-achieving, several were recently promoted). Remember, although you are interviewing the candidate, they are also interviewing you and the company.

EXAMPLE 4-1
SAMPLE BEHAVIORAL QUESTIONS FOR A MANAGEMENT POSITION INTERVIEW

- Each member of a management team contributes unique strengths and weaknesses. For the last or current leadership team you belonged to, describe the unique skills and talents that you brought to the team beyond your functional knowledge. Describe the ways in which you relied on other team members for coaching and advice.
- Tell me about a time when you and a peer leader invented something together or created a new process or practice. How did it come about and what did you do to bring out the best in your peer?
- Describe a time when you asserted yourself at a regular leadership team meeting. What was the situation? What did you say? What were the results?

- Describe the two contributions you made in the last year that you are most proud of? How have these contributions helped the company?
- Beyond your functional projects and tasks, in what ways have you helped the company improve its ability to manage, execute, and react to change?
- Tell me about a peer with whom you have had the most difficulty working? What made it difficult? What did you do about it? What were the results?
- Over the last year, what was the largest problem you had to solve? How did you approach it? What did you do? What were the results?
- Describe your leadership and management style. How do you ensure everyone on your team is working on the right stuff? How do you communicate? What's your belief about what makes people perform their best?
- Tell me about a time when you were the most satisfied, energized, and productive at work. What aspects of the job made you feel that way? How often have you felt that way?

Asking effective questions is not the most important part of the interview, however. Listening and assessing each candidate's response is how you determine fit. Listening means that you allow each candidate to answer fully. Don't interrupt or think about the next question on your list. To assess the responses, you'll need to compare your job fit criteria with what each candidate says. Were they able to share specific examples that highlighted their unique contributions or were the stories and examples more general or broad? Example 4-2 offers a few specific examples of what to look for.

You are making hiring decisions that will change lives and affect your team's short- and long-term effectiveness. It's important to consider the significance of what candidates are sharing with you, as well as what they don't say. For example, if a candidate never mentions people, teams, collaboration, or relationships, it might be a red flag that they prefer individual work. Ask follow-up questions until you are comfortable with your assessment of fit.

POINTER

Listening and assessing each candidate's response to your questions is how you determine fit.

EXAMPLE 4-2
TIPS FOR ASSESSING BEHAVIORAL QUESTIONS

You're Interviewing For	Say	Determine
Teamwork and Collaboration Skills	Give me an example of a time when your work group completed a difficult project. What was your role and the outcome?	• Did the candidate give you a feel for how well they worked as a member of a team? • Do they value collaboration and being open to other's ideas?
Communication or Conflict Resolution	Tell me about a time you disagreed with a co-worker or supervisor, and what did you do in the situation?	• Did they avoid conflict or resolve the conflict constructively? • Did they consider the other person's point of view? • Did they own their role in the situation? • Did they use effective listening and communication skills to resolve the situation?
Engagement	Tell me about a time when you were the most satisfied, energized, and productive at work. What aspects of the job made you feel that way? How often have you felt that way?	• Does the type of work that engaged them previously exist in this job? • Were the aspects of the job that engaged them reflective of meaningful and productive work?

STEP 4

Assessing interview question responses is not easy! There are so many factors that can make a strong candidate seem like a poor fit, and unqualified candidates look like a better fit than they are. Here are a few dynamics to consider:

- Some candidates interview well (they sound good, seem confident) but say the wrong things in terms of fit. Other candidates aren't natural interviewees, but the substance of their answers is better in terms of fit.
- Some candidates are storytellers who make it difficult to evaluate specific competencies (other than storytelling).
- Some candidates answer, very effectively, questions *other than* the ones you asked.
- Candidate interviews might occur over several days or weeks, making remembering and comparing responses more challenging.
- As interviewers, we bring our preferences and individual styles to the conversation and sometimes this makes the process more challenging. For example, if we have a bias for action and accountability but need to assess for teaming and collaboration. Also, if both the interviewer (you) and interviewee are storytellers, you might not learn enough information about each other to make a decision!

There are many reasons why determining fit is challenging. But if you take the time to carefully define fit criteria and thoughtfully interview candidates, you will have the best chance to make great hiring decisions.

If no candidate is a great fit, keep looking. Don't hire someone because they are available and convenient. This won't benefit the organization or the person hired. Managers who are picky about the people they bring onto their team will enjoy better results than their less selective peers.

Hire for Fit Interview Process Tips

Your interview process will vary based on your organization's standards, the job level, and type of work, but here's are suggestions that apply in most situations:

- Before
  - Define fit criteria.
  - Create a list of behavioral questions.

- Review resume and interview questions.
- Schedule the interview in quiet meeting room and block your calendar to allow for a good discussion.

- During
  - Greet candidate.
  - Share that you'll be using behavior-based questions and asking for examples.
  - Ask questions and follow-up questions as needed.
  - Take effective notes about the candidate's responses.
  - Close and share next steps.
- After
  - Review your notes, assess fit.
  - Seek feedback from other interviewers.
  - Conduct additional interviews if needed.
  - Share feedback with HR partner.
  - Make a hiring decision.

STEP 4

Each hiring decision is an opportunity to strengthen your team's skills, make-up, and potential. I always loved the selection process and loved the feeling I got when I changed lives for the better. That's what offering someone a job does. It's a beautiful thing, and I hope you take your time and enjoy the process.

Onboard Well

Rejoice and celebrate! You have a new team member who will bring energy and talent to the work environment. And it's important that both your new hire and your team see your enthusiasm. You want your new hire to feel special, welcome, and needed. With every new hire, you communicate again—to all team members—the behaviors and talents that you seek and value. You reinforce your vision of excellence (another reason to never settle, as doing so dilutes your definition of excellence because actions speak louder than words).

POINTER

The faster you can help new employees transition from feeling like an outsider to feeling like an insider, the better.

Let's imagine you've selected a new employee, whom we'll call Brad. Awesome! Now it's time to onboard Brad, the final part of step 4. Onboarding is more than getting Brad's badge, introducing him to the team, buying him a pizza lunch, and telling him to do great work. Oh wait, you weren't thinking pizza? I know, you likely didn't receive great onboarding and you turned out OK. No computer login for the first week? That sets a tone. And maybe no one bought you lunch or even told you where the employee cafeteria was located. I get it. But before you throw Brad to the dog-eat-dog world you might've experienced, let's explore the importance of his initial days and weeks on the job:

- The first day is critical. Consider Brad's first day as an opportunity to begin the relationship-building process.
- The first week sets the tone and enables Brad to see what the work environment is really like.
- Within the first month, Brad will have formed a perception of his new job.
- Within the first two months, Brad will know if he's made the right decision.

You took great care to select Brad for your open role and your team needs Brad's contribution to succeed. Don't waste all your efforts by chasing him away. Brad's onboarding experience will have a major impact on whether he stays or leaves for another job.

On the one hand, this makes perfect sense—we all want to feel welcomed and valued, and starting a new job can be scary. We are reliant on others and it's upsetting if we are left to fend for ourselves. But there's more at play here. Social sciences researchers have been studying something called *job embeddedness* and how it affects a new employee's intention to leave and ultimately whether they stay. What is job embeddedness? I like this definition from the article "Why People Stay: Using Job Embeddedness to Predict Voluntary Turnover":

> Job embeddedness is like a net or a web in which one can become "stuck." One who is highly embedded has

many links that are close together. . . . The content of the parts may vary considerably, suggesting that one can be enmeshed or embedded in many *different* ways. (Mitchell et al. 2001)

The word *stuck* here is referring to something positive. It's the degree to which Brad builds connections that make his job and your company stickier—harder to leave. Along with ensuring that Brad learns his new job and has the resources he needs to do great work (both of which are important), onboarding should help Brad build connections that increase his embeddedness. The faster you help new employees transition from feeling like an outsider to feeling like an insider, the better. The faster onboarded employees feel welcome and prepared for their jobs, the faster they will be able to contribute to the organization's success.

There's another benefit of job embeddedness—the more embedded Brad is, the better he will perform. So, in addition to getting Brad's badge and system logins, help him build new connections. Workplace connections will help Brad figure out how things work and how he can get his job tasks done. If Brad needs help figuring out the intranet, he can ask his buddy or the IT department if you've introduced him to them (and they will be more eager to help him too). We can more confidently do our jobs when embeddedness is high. Tool 4-1 lists several ideas for improving job embeddedness during a new employee's initial weeks on the job.

You have a chance to improve the strength and effectiveness of your team each time you fill an open position. The decision to hire affects you and your team for years, so it is important that you hire for fit and onboard for success. It might be one of the more time-consuming processes you encounter, but rightly so.

POINTER

Onboarding is more than getting Brad's badge, introducing him to the team, buying him a pizza lunch, and telling him to do great work.

TOOL 4-1
TIPS FOR ONBOARDING TO BUILD JOB EMBEDDEDNESS

- Introduce the new employee to the team and other key colleagues in an informal setting.
- Assign the employee a buddy on the team to serve as an onboarding mentor.
- Schedule 30-minute one-on-ones with five to 10 co-workers the employee will work with most.
- Spend time, one-on-one, going over the new employee's job duties, goals, and common questions about the workplace. Do this over several meetings.
- Invite the employee to any meetings that will help them build knowledge about the department or company.
- Share information about informal clubs or community events that the company is involved in (such as the annual Heart Walk or book clubs).
- Share what you love about the organization, why you do this work, and what you're most excited about in the next year.
- Ask team members to give the new employee tours of the workplace. This can be split into several, shorter tours led by different team members.
- Find ways to use the employee's experience and skills for a quick win.
- Check in often and encourage the employee to ask questions.

Building ACCEL Skills

The management techniques we've explored in step 4, "Hire for Fit and Onboard for Success," will help you build the following ACCEL skills:

- **Accountability:** The skills that you practice as part of step 4 will support your ability to become a more accountable manager, because hiring decisions call upon you to take action in ways that will improve team results in the short and long term. There are accountability steps related to selection and onboarding that you'll hone as you develop.
- **Engagement:** The selection and onboarding process requires you to involve and inspire team members and new hires.

And the onboarding process will help you build skills in engagement related to building relationships and workplace connections.

- **Listening and assessing:** The selection process uses your listening and assessment skills in important ways. As you practice good interviewing techniques, you will hone your ability to listen deeply and make selection decisions based on your assessment of each candidate's interview responses.

Your Turn

Take the time and initiative to reflect on your current practices and determine how you can better hire for fit and onboard for success.

- Ask yourself:
  - ○ Are you taking enough time with candidates?
  - ○ Are you building relationships during the interview process?
  - ○ Have you defined fit criteria?
  - ○ Is your onboarding program building job embeddedness?
- Evaluate the effectiveness of your last few hires. Would you have made the same decision if you'd known then what you know about the employee now?
- If you have some work to do to improve your hiring, ask your HR partner for coaching that will help you make the next recruiting process deeper and more detailed.
- Take some time to define the job, culture, and team fit criteria for an open position.
- Ask your HR partner to help you create an amazing list of behavioral interview questions for the job title you recruit for most often.

The Next Step

In this chapter you learned ways you can ensure new hires are a great fit for your team and are onboarded well. For step 5, you'll learn how to use pull motivation to build an engaging workplace.

Step 5
Use Pull Versus Push Motivation

Overview

- Distinguish intrinsic and extrinsic motivation.
- Use the right motivational tools.
- Create more pull in the workplace.
- Model engagement.

Here's a scary thought: Engagement is a gift that you might not have earned.

Pause.

Engagement is a gift that you might not have earned.

It's true, but fear not; step 5 will help you improve employee *engagement* and be the kind of manager your team wants to work for. No, my advice will not include handing out cupcakes, but feel free to do that because everyone loves cupcakes.

But seriously, let's talk about engagement. Did you notice that the name of this step does not contain the word engagement? That's because engagement is not something you can do or control. Engagement happens when employees are motivated to give discretionary effort to a task. These moments transcend the basic employee–boss relationship and show a higher level of connection and commitment. It's lovely when it happens, and it is a required ingredient for employees to do their best work. That's why every company in the free world is launching employee engagement initiatives and paying trillions of dollars to consultants to proctor 40-minute surveys that employees take because their managers bribed them with delicious cupcakes.

Sorry, do I sound a jaded? I love cupcakes, but I'm not a fan of using surveys to force managers to behave better because they fear what a bad score might mean for their career. It doesn't work that way, anyway, and you'll learn more about why and what you can do to affect employee engagement in this step.

Distinguish Intrinsic and Extrinsic Motivation

Before we explore managerial techniques, it's important that we clarify key terms. Your success will depend on your understanding of them. There are two types of motivators:

- Extrinsic motivator—something happening external to the person with the intent of improving motivation. For example, "I'll give you a $1,000 bonus if you meet your productivity goal." Extrinsic motivation is behavior that is driven by external rewards, such as recognition, money, notoriety, or praise.

- Intrinsic motivator—something happening internal to the person that motivates them. For example, Sally was determined to find the error in the process because she loved solving tough problems. Intrinsic motivation is behavior that is driven for its own sake and personal rewards.

Think about your current company and department. Can you list the extrinsic and intrinsic motivators? Use Exercise 5-1 to practice distinguishing motivators. (You can find my answers to this exercise at the end of the chapter.)

Extrinsic and intrinsic motivators are neither good nor bad; both are useful and alive in our organizations. But if you want to improve engagement, you'll need to tap into and ignite intrinsic motivation.

EXERCISE 5-1
EXTRINSIC OR INTRINSIC MOTIVATOR?

For each of the following scenarios, determine whether what's driving the behavior is extrinsic or intrinsic motivation (or both).

Scenario	Extrinsic	Intrinsic
1. Emma comes back from a training class where she learned how to use a cool new software program. She immediately creates a sample report using the new software.		
2. Emma's manager offers her the opportunity to take on the role of project team leader. She brainstorms things she'll need to do to prepare for the team launch.		
3. Emma's manager assigns a goal for the project team and reviews expectations for each level of performance (e.g., meet expectations and exceed expectation). Emma brainstorms things she'll need to do to achieve the highest rating.		
4. Emma knows she's not supposed to work from home. However, she creates a presentation for her team launch after putting the kids to bed because she wants the launch meeting to go well.		
5. Emma's manager tells the team they'll get a pizza party if they maintain their perfect safety record for three months. Emma makes sure she wears her protective gear.		
6. Emma receives an email from her manager critical of her for missing something. Emma drops what she's doing to address her manager's concern and fix the problem.		

Use the Right Motivational Tools

Perhaps you've heard the saying, "Don't bring a knife to a gun fight." It's important to use the correct tools (but please don't shoot or stab anyone). You wouldn't use knitting needles to sew a quilt or serve soup on a plate. And it wouldn't make sense to pump up your bicycle tires with a cotton ball.

While these examples seem obvious, we commonly mess this up when it comes to motivational tools. Here's a true story that illustrates this: I asked a senior leader what her organization's goals were for the coming year. She told me that one goal was to increase ownership of the strategic plan at all levels of the organization. She wanted every employee to internalize and demonstrate ownership for their part in making the strategies come to fruition. I then asked her what their action plan was for making this goal happen. She listed several items like these:

- Conduct mandatory monthly meetings to review strategic plan elements with staff.
- Cascade the overall goal to employees' goals.
- Require every staff meeting to include a review of departmental goals and performance to those goals.

I said to the leader, "You're bringing a knife to a gun fight." Well no, I didn't say that, but could've. I told her that her action plan wouldn't work as she intended. This leader was extremely bright and well-regarded in the organization, but the look on her face told me she did not understand. To her credit, the actions she and her team had agreed upon were reasonable, good-to-do things, they just had little chance of creating ownership. They weren't designed to produce those types of behavior.

Ownership is intrinsically driven. You can't force someone to own—in their heart or mind—anything. You can hold people accountable because accountability is extrinsically driven. In my example, the leader's actions were extrinsically driven. Do you see that? Something is happening external to the person with the intent on improving motivation for owning the strategic plan. Figure 5-1 presents a diagram that might help illustrate this important point.

FIGURE 5-1
HOW TO SELECT MOTIVATIONAL TOOLS

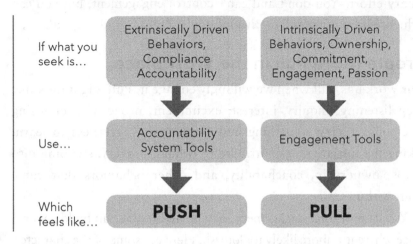

If what you seek is...	Extrinsically Driven Behaviors, Compliance Accountability	Intrinsically Driven Behaviors, Ownership, Commitment, Engagement, Passion
Use...	Accountability System Tools	Engagement Tools
Which feels like...	**PUSH**	**PULL**

STEP **5**

Going back to my example, the leader's goal was to increase employee ownership of the strategic plan. Ownership is an intrinsically driven behavior. The action plan they created contained accountability system tools (mandatory meetings, employee goals, and meeting requirements). Knife at a gun fight.

Think through a few examples of your own to test the diagram. Imagine that your manager told you that she'd like you to be more engaged and then shared with you a goal regarding engagement that she was adding to your performance metrics. How would you feel? First, handing out engagement goals is a dumb thing to do—that's like bringing a marshmallow to a gun fight. It doesn't work; not by a long shot. If I want you to be a more engaged employee, as your manager I need to use engagement tools. These will feel like pull.

POINTER

Engagement tools feel like pull.

And that's why this step is called "Use Pull Versus Push Motivation." For example, in Exercise 5-1, Emma is pulled into her work, for the sake of that work, because she's motived from within. This is the place where discretionary effort comes from, and it's how we help catalyze the best performance.

We're using some different sounding words in this chapter. Managers create environments, catalyze performance, and inspire extraordinary effort. You don't and can't control engagement, but you can influence it by using pull motivation tools. Pull . . . pull . . . pull. . . .

Create More Pull in the Workplace

Our work has pull when we willingly engage it. Pull might look like deep listening, inquiry, interest, excitement, proactivity, choosing to change, trying something new with gusto, eagerness to learn, taking the initiative to contribute to others, bravery, stepping into chaos, ownership, coachability, and other behaviors that come from within.

You cannot force engagement to happen, but you can build a workplace where it is more likely to flourish. Here are some of the characteristics of a workplace that supports high employee engagement:

- Employees feel challenged. They have interesting problems to solve.
- Employees use their strengths in the service of meaningful goals.
- Employees feel connected to their work, team, and the company (high embeddedness, as in step 4).
- Employees feel cared for (step 2), valued, and special.
- Employees have the opportunity to collaborate and partner with peers to solve important problems or implement worthy projects.
- Employees grow professionally and personally.
- Employees have some control over their work; they can make choices that affect their work.
- Employees believe their work has meaning and is important.
- Employees have fun at work.

Want to know how you can create more pull in the workplace? After all, pull is not something you can push. The good news is that creating pull does not require you to implement a long or complicated process. You can do it in many small ways. And you don't even need to buy cupcakes. That would be an extrinsic motivator, right?

To create more pull in the workplace, add new workplace elements that provoke or evoke your employees' inner motivation to the things you are doing now. There's a list of these elements in Exercise 5-2. For example, you can use your morning or beginning of shift rounding (or huddles) to ask your employees for ways you can help remove challenges or barriers they are facing. If you show interest and take initiative to make things better, your employees will smile, high-five you, and feel less work-related stress. This would be an example of adding the "make things better" element to your regular communication practices. Take a minute to brainstorm more ways and situations in which you can create more pull (Exercise 5-2).

POINTER

You cannot force engagement to happen, but you can build a workplace where it is more likely to flourish.

STEP **5**

EXERCISE 5-2
MANAGEMENT PRACTICES THAT CREATE PULL IN THE WORKPLACE

Workplace Element	Where Can You Use This?
Evokes a sense of pride	
Is fascinating, interesting, or unique	
Makes things better	
Creates a strong sense of urgency for something deemed worthy	
Improves relationships	
Celebrates the best in people	
Expands capabilities and confidence	
Offers a worthy challenge	
Is fun	

Did you notice that I inserted the word *worthy* a couple times in Exercise 5-2? That's an important distinction. Employees love a challenge and will pull into one as long as it represents something that is worthy of their efforts. If you double their production goals, thinking it is a good challenge, well then you won't see much in the way of pull. Similarly, pet projects that seem like a waste of time to most people won't get much pull. Compliance, perhaps, but not pull.

You can create more pull by making small but impactful changes to the things you already do. Let's use the example of your next team meeting to illustrate. Example 5-1 fills in the chart from Exercise 5-2 with ideas for applying the elements that improve pull at your next staff meeting.

Did reviewing Example 5-1 give you any ideas? Try going through the exercise with other situations, such as huddles, goal setting, rounding, or training. However, I've got a few caveats: First, although the focus of this step is on creating pull by igniting intrinsic motivation, I am not suggesting that accountability systems (extrinsically driven) are bad. We'll discuss accountability in step 6. It's another tool that produces different, but also important, outcomes. As managers, you have many tools.

Second, creating pull is not a science—*if you do X, you will not always get Y.* When it comes to engagement, you are not in control. Engagement is an intrinsically driven behavior that occurs when we pull ourselves into the work. But the situation that elicits pull for me might be different than what motivates you. And it might change. There are some common triggers and conditions that tend to evoke intrinsic motivation more often, and managers who use these will see more employee engagement. And there are common elements that make the difference for many of us.

Before you plan your staff meeting, huddles, one-on-ones, rounding, or work plans, review the management practices that create pull and determine ways you can make the workplace a bit more motivating. Small actions, practiced consistently, will yield better results than twice yearly grand gestures.

EXAMPLE 5-1

MANAGEMENT PRACTICES THAT CREATE PULL IN THE WORKPLACE

Workplace Element	At the Team Meeting
Celebrates the best in people	Openly acknowledge people and groups. Use the meeting as a forum to share recognition.
Is fascinating, interesting, or unique	Share a video or short article about what's going on that's new and amazing in your team's functional area.
Evokes a sense of pride	Invite someone from another department or senior leadership to share how the team's work affects the community. Share what the organization does that is best in class compared with competitors.
Makes things better	Dedicate a portion of the meeting to allow team members to improve some aspect of their work that is troublesome to them.
Creates a strong sense of urgency for something deemed worthy	Be open about potential ramifications for work issues. Share long-term goals and where the market is heading.
Improves relationships	Take time at each meeting to help members get to know one another by breaking into smaller task groups or by opening the meeting with an interesting ice-breaker exercise.
Expands capabilities and confidence	Take time to build new skills, perhaps inviting someone from another department to teach the team something or having team members teach something to one another.
Offers a worthy challenge	Ask team members what they'd like to accomplish in the coming months or year. Share opportunities to contribute to the organization in a greater way. Allow team members to play on other teams for select projects.
Is fun	Make the meeting enjoyable, even if you have many important agenda items. Bring some lightness to the meeting. Greet team members warmly, and thank them for their participation. Laugh a little when you can.

STEP 5

Model Engagement

I could end every chapter with the suggestion that you need to model the behaviors that you seek, but it's particularly worth noting for this step. At the root of engagement is energy—an energy that comes from within and that expands or contracts based on intrinsic motivation. That energy can be contagious.

POINTER

Your most power-ful tool for improv-ing employee engagement may be inside you.

When we see a heartwarming story about people helping the homeless, it usually evokes within us the desire to do more for people. When we see someone having fun breaking down empty boxes, we'll likely join in. When we watch a co-worker get absorbed in solving a persistent problem, we're often inspired to dig in with them. Engagement itself is a workplace element that generates pull.

So remember, show your passion for your work. Share the fascinating aspects of your job. Have some fun! Find the inner fire that motivates your discretionary effort and be that fully engaged manager your employees want to be around. Your most powerful tool for improving employee engagement may be inside you. Let it out.

Building ACCEL Skills

The management techniques we've explored in step 5, "Use Pull Versus Push Motivation," will help you build the following ACCEL skills:

- **Collaboration:** The skills you are practicing to create more pull will also help you build collaboration. The best collaboration happens when team members are actively engaged in the work, so the fundamentals of intrinsic motivation also apply here.
- **Engagement:** This step is squarely focused on helping you build the skills to improve employee engagement through increasing pull and modeling engagement.
- **Listening and assessing:** As you create a work environment with more pull, you'll be listening deeply to determine what

best motivates your team members. And you'll assess and adjust your managerial practices to continually hone your efforts to improve engagement.

Your Turn

Here are a few suggestions for ways you can practice what you've learned in this chapter:

- Learn how to better distinguish intrinsic and extrinsic motivation by observing what team members do and assessing what's driving their actions.
- Take some time to consider the goals you have for your department and assess whether your actions are aligned with the types of behavioral changes you seek (use extrinsic tools to produce extrinsically driven outcomes and vice versa).
- Review Exercise 5-2 at the beginning of each week. Choose one element to focus on for the week, and then try a different element the following week.
- Practice tapping into your intrinsic motivation. Notice what works for you and consider whether similar approaches might help your employees.

Here are my answers to Exercise 5-1:

1. Intrinsic
2. Intrinsic
3. Extrinsic
4. Mostly intrinsic, but also some extrinsic
5. Extrinsic
6. Extrinsic

The Next Step

In this chapter we focused on improving engagement, which is intrinsically driven and characterized by pull. Step 6 will help you increase accountability, an extrinsically driven behavior.

Step 6

Reinforce and Reward the Nonnegotiables

Overview

- Recognize accountability pitfalls.
- Determine the "gottas"—expectations you are willing to require.
- Ensure team members know where they stand.
- Demonstrate courage to reinforce expectations.

There's rocky road ice cream, and then there's steamed broccoli. Hiking through a redwood forest and thorny yard work. Shiny new lipstick and waxy dental floss. There's employee engagement and accountability.

People often talk about engagement using romantic and idyllic terms. It's something that is fun, exciting, and special. Heck, step 5 (the chapter on *pull*) was pretty darn magical and optimistic. There's something about tapping into people's hearts and minds that makes us melt with purpose-driven satisfaction. *Give me more!*

Accountability, on the other hand, is often described quite differently. In sterile terms. As a necessary evil. Something that is important to do, but undesirable. Something many managers dread (because it's perceived as hard and unwelcome), but that their bosses obsess over (because it's perceived as *the key* to great performance). Both perceptions are wrong, by the way. I get that there's a different aura surrounding accountability and acknowledge there's a kernel of truth to our darker view of it. I'd say it's a little bit like people telling you to *floss your teeth* or *eat less and exercise more*. Blah! And it is, after all, an extrinsically based managerial system that has no potential to produce extraordinary performance. That's no knock on extrinsic motivators, they serve a purpose but they're not designed to affect intrinsically driven behaviors (for more information, refer to the last step's "Use the Right Motivational Tools" segment).

Even so, accountability is absolutely crucial for organizational success and sanity. And it can be a positive and powerful managerial tool when used with focus and deliberateness. In step 6, I'm inviting you to take on a decidedly hopeful view of accountability and how you use it to improve performance and complement your efforts to jack up employee engagement. *Accountability* is not a four-letter word. In fact, it can be a liberating source of organizational peace and prosperity. Really!

Recognize Accountability Pitfalls

Perhaps what I just wrote surprised you. Perhaps my description does not ring true when squared up with your experiences. If so, you've likely dealt with one or more accountability failures. Like many managerial ~~weapons~~ tools, accountability is often misunderstood and misused. Tool 6-1 lists several common pitfalls you should avoid and what's really true for each situation.

Have you seen these pitfalls in action? Perhaps you've perpetuated them yourself. It's OK, don't beat yourself up too much; these are common mistakes and you can easily tune up your accountability practices. At the core of these pitfalls is emotional mental garbage and good intentions. Mental garbage occurs because we—as humans—don't like holding people accountable. It's negative, and we want to be a well-liked manager. It's uncomfortable to talk to employees about where they've fallen short and it's also often tough to tell employees they've done well.

TOOL 6-1
ACCOUNTABILITY PITFALLS AND TRUTHS

Pitfall	Truth
Looking "out there" to performers for accountability. If you said or heard that *employees need to be more accountable,* you've seen this pitfall in action. Sure, personal accountability is a thing. It's great, and we all ought to aspire to holding ourselves to high standards. But as a manager, personal accountability is not something you can change (except yours).	**Accountability is a management system. If you have an accountability problem, you have a management problem.** As a manager, you can set expectations, communicate them, reward those who meet your expectations, and hold those who don't to account. If you want to create a more accountable workplace, one or more of these steps needs to be improved.
Defining many standards and managing few. It is common to set expectations and standards for dozens of behaviors and tasks with the hope that communicating them once or twice per year will be enough to ensure employees do what they're supposed to. It is also common that managers then fail to actively manage these standards, rendering the accountability system a charade.	**Accountability requires monitoring and follow-through.** The secret to accountability is consistency. Most managers have neither the time nor the interest needed to hold employees accountable for a long list of desired behaviors. It is better to set only those standards that you're willing to act upon. This is one reason why long employee surveys are viewed as a waste of time. They produce much more feedback than management is willing or able to follow up on.
Managing accountability measures in a lopsided, mostly negative, manner. If employees fail to meet a basic expectation, they should be counseled and face appropriate consequences. But what about the employee—maybe even the same employee in a different situation— who does the right things? Many managers ignore compliant behavior because they believe that's just part of the job.	**Accountability systems use extrinsic motivation—in the form of positive and negative consequences—to ensure performance standards.** When managers spend more time on deficiencies than efficiencies, they ignore two realities: • in an extrinsic motivation system, good behavior needs reinforcement • it's a problem if poor performance receives more attention than good performance.

Most managers have good intentions regarding accountability. They honestly believe the standards they set and communicate. They fully expect to measure and follow through. And they want to dish out just as much positive reinforcement as negative. They really, really believe they can and should do this. And then the enormity of doing accountability well sets in and, along with all the other to-do items, becomes unmanageable. Some rationalize that struggling employees need them more than the others. Others convince themselves that basic expectations should not need positive reinforcement even though they know better based on their personal experience.

It's important to come to terms and be comfortable with what it means to use an extrinsic motivation system. It's about power and rank. Let's not paint a river rock blue and call it a gem. As the manager, it's your job to hold your employees accountable. You set the standard, you measure performance, you dish out rewards and punishments. You are in charge; the employees are not. I know this feels hard to say or grasp, but this is what it means to use extrinsic motivation. Same goes with pay raises, bonuses, suspensions, and terminations. You have the power to use these tools to get something in return.

The best way to use accountability systems is to be open and real about what they are and what they are not. To be more matter-of-fact about your role and theirs, acknowledge that it's weird and uncomfortable to use power and position in this way, but it's an important tool to ensure the basic foundation for performance. (Hint: Employees know this is your job to do, just like you know your boss should hold you accountable.) Reassure them you're going to focus on the standards that really matter and that you'll follow through. Express your hope and expectation that with a strong, focused accountability system ensuring the basics are covered, the team will be able to spend more time on work that brings out their interests and strengths. With an effective accountability system, you can reduce the mental garbage and create a more relaxed and fun workplace. Really! It starts with defining the standards you're willing to manage.

POINTER

With an effective accountability system, you can reduce the mental garbage and create a more relaxed and fun workplace.

Determine the "Gottas"

Read your employee handbook, strategic plan, corporate values, and job descriptions and you'll see hundreds of expectations. They're all valid and important. But you can't pretend to track and follow up with all of these standards. And it's a farce to clump them together with single signature acknowledgment sheets and call it good. Determining the "gottas" means defining the standards that you are willing to manage—really manage.

Here's a true story that illustrates my point. I was working with the leadership team of a small travel company to conduct a succession plan. I facilitated a discussion where the leaders assessed the performance and potential of each key team member. When we got to one woman, I'll call her Brenda, the conversation took an unexpected turn. The leaders agreed that her potential to move into a broader role in the future was medium (on a high-medium-low scale). When describing her potential, they recognized her technical skills, but several mentioned that she had major challenges in terms of social prowess. They agreed she was not meeting their expectations in the areas of teaming and communication. Truth be told, people did not like working with her, and she had periodic meltdowns at work. I pulled up her employee record and performance evaluations. No disciplinary actions and she had received "exceeds expectations" ratings on her last three reviews. She'd also received higher-than-average salary increases. Unfortunately, none of this surprised me—it's a common situation. Here's how our conversation went (paraphrasing):

- **Me:** It appears Brenda is not only meeting but also exceeding your expectations regarding communications.
- **Leaders:** No, she is not. We've sat Brenda down to talk with her after each at-work implosion.
- **Me:** OK, that's a good start; what happened then?
- **Leaders:** She was nicer for a few days and then went back to being her usual Brenda. She's got important technical

knowledge. We can't lose her. If she leaves, it would be hard to find someone to take her place.

- **Me:** OK, all valid considerations, but not the point. Expectations are defined and redefined every day with your words and actions. I don't doubt for one moment that you honestly feel that Brenda should improve her teaming and communication skills. But your actions are saying that this is not really required. And by the way, this is evident to everyone, not just you and me, and might be eroding your overall team collaboration.
- **Leaders:** What are we supposed to do?
- **Me:** Choose what you're willing to manage, but don't pretend that you have established expectations around effective teaming because you haven't. Your actual standard, in practice, is that you don't have to be a good team member if you have valued technical skills. Brenda is meeting that standard with no difficulty.
- **Leaders:** . . . [*Look around at each other and sigh.*]

I'm sharing this story because it is both dramatic and common. As managers, the senior team has the responsibility to establish and manage basic expectations. And in the case of Brenda, they chose to forgo holding her accountable aside from a few toothless discussions. She was meeting their expectations, and through their inaction the leaders lowered the behavioral standards for everyone.

In the real world, there are often employees with skill sets that you might believe you can't lose. But be clear about the consequences and more deliberate about managing based on those choices.

So how do you go about determining the "gottas"—those standards that you are willing to manage fully? My recommendation is to start with a small and focused list of behavioral requirements and performance metrics that you are willing and able to monitor and manage. You can expand it later if you have the managerial capacity. Example 6-1 presents my short list.

EXAMPLE 6-1

LISA'S BASIC EXPECTATIONS

The "Gottas"	Why required?
Be an effective team member. Treat people with respect, be helpful, have a positive demeanor, collaborate well, seek to resolve conflicts, be inclusive, ask for and accept peer coaching, share in credit and responsibility.	It is a fundamental job requirement that we work together in the service of organizational goals. Our success depends on our ability to work together.
Demonstrate integrity. Do what you say you will do. Keep your promises and be reliable.	We need to be able to trust that we'll each do our part because our work is interdependent. A delay in one area affects others. Errors can reverberate and cause additional mistakes.
Take the initiative to make things better. If you see something is wrong, fix it or say something to those who can. If you have an idea for how we can do something better, share it while providing full information.	Every team member needs to help us see and solve problems and improve our practices.
Basic job responsibility 1. For each position, select a fundamental job duty that is nonnegotiable.	We each have a role with specific requirements that are important to the department's success. Share the specific reason that each "gotta" is a nonnegotiable.
Basic job responsibility 2. For each position, select a fundamental job duty that is nonnegotiable.	

What do you think about my list? It's heavy on behaviors, which I think is appropriate. Think about the issues that cause problems for most teams:

- an inability to work with others
- not doing what was promised
- holding up processes due to lateness or inefficiencies.

I like this list of "gottas" because it is manageable. This is a key point—it's manageable. The "gottas" are those standards that you are willing and able to follow through on. Please don't say you're going to hold employees accountable for a laundry list of standards that you have no way of managing. Focus on the few and be consistent. Observe and measure those things and deliver the appropriate consequences for good and poor performance. My list includes expectations that are important enough that I'm willing to get past any discomfort associated with holding team members accountable. And, importantly, these are behaviors that I'm committed to role modeling—holding myself accountable.

POINTER

The "gottas" are those standards that you are willing and able to follow through on and manage.

Once you've determined the "gottas," ensure that every employee is crystal clear about them. You can communicate these during one-on-ones or along with grand slam goals (step 3). Accountability standards and grand slam goals are different things, for sure; and all the better that you discuss and clarify both during the same meeting to ensure understanding.

TEAMING *Is* a Core Job Task, Not Something Else

I was talking with a leader whose team is struggling. Many of the team members act like bullies and have been seen yelling, swearing, and gossiping. This leader also mentioned that *all* his team members were good performers in terms of their job tasks. When I looked surprised, he said that they had a separate and slower discipline process for dealing with people who did not demonstrate the corporate values (which is where he classified the teaming behaviors).

In other words, he did not consider teaming behaviors to be "job tasks." I suggested that this was at the core of his issue and that he move expectations regarding teaming into the category of basic job tasks and out of the nice-to-have category. Work is a team endeavor and yelling at someone is a failing of a fundamental performance expectation.

In your workplace, are teaming expectations held to the same level of importance and accountability as technical job tasks? I think they should be. More teams fail to meet their goals due to teaming issues than because of poor technical skills. If you want to be goal-oriented, you need to be team-development oriented.

And here is one more question/challenge. What kind of a team member are you? Do your employees consider you a role model of great teaming? We do employee engagement surveys and we always ask about this. It is very common to get results that tell us that managers are not playing well with each other and are not setting a good tone for their teams. You might not be a great team member if:

- You are over-controlling.
- You avoid your peers because you don't want to deal with them.
- You talk unflatteringly about your peers.
- You impede progress during meetings or conversations (watch for people who check out).
- You are passive-aggressive (say "yes" but mean "no").
- You are no fun to work with—for whatever reason(s).

Be the bigger person. Extend the olive branch. Be a joy! Bring donuts without being asked. But most important, enable progress and visibly support peers. You will live longer (less stress), your peers will live longer (less stress), and your company will live longer (better results).

Ensure Team Members Know Where They Stand

Once you've defined and communicated the "gottas," the next thing is to make sure team members are clear about how they are doing. Remember Brenda? She knew that her moods could get sour at times. She knew her managers wished she was less cranky, and she was aware that she caused conflict; her manager talked to her about these issues. She did not grasp that being an effective team member was a fundamental job duty. She did not realize her career could be negatively affected by her dysfunctional behavior. And she certainly did not know that she might lose her job if she didn't improve.

You might argue that a reasonable person should assume these consequences, but remember, an accountability system is a management tool. It is the manager's job to make sure employees know where they stand—really know—and what that might mean. There are two parts to doing this:

- Measure performance against requirements.
- Share the metrics.

I know what you're thinking. . . . How do I measure teaming expectations? It's true that it is easier to track timely report completion than positive demeanor. I think this is one reason why teaming issues are often overlooked and allowed to let slide. But if you want accountability, you'll need to be able to determine and tell employees how they're doing. Luckily, this is totally doable. Behavioral expectations are measurable in a few different ways:

- **Observational:** Your direct observations of team members in various workplace situations. Be sure to share specific behaviors and impacts, not general impressions.
  - Don't say: Brenda, you had a bad attitude during the meeting today.
  - Say instead: Brenda, during the meeting you repeatedly cut off other team members [offer examples], and looked perturbed when others shared alternatives. This had a negative impact on our discussion, discouraged others from participating, and might've prevented us from solving an important problem together.
  - Don't say: Brenda, you did pretty well today at the meeting. Keep it up.
  - Say instead: Brenda, you asked several really great questions today, for example [include examples], and you seemed open to and thankful for the input you received. You helped our discussion be more productive.

- **Feedback:** The positive and negative observations from others. Ask for specifics akin to the previous point. It's fine and great if people share, "I like working with Brenda," or "I don't like working with Brenda," but you can't reinforce (reward or punish) the performance unless you have the details.
- **Quantitative:** Results from team surveys. You might decide to use brief surveys to seek feedback from team members for the "gottas." The key to surveys is ensuring the question/item is specific enough to be helpful.
  - Not effective: Please rate Brenda as a team member on a scale of 1-10.
  - Better survey item: Brenda has sought my opinion and input about a project or process challenge.
  - Better survey item: Brenda shares relevant information with me.

When you first roll out your short list of the "gottas," you might choose to focus on one or two per month—letting everyone know you're doing this—to increase the attention and awareness on each behavior. And it would be even better if you reminded the team of your expectation at the beginning of team meetings and huddles. If it's important (the "gottas" are by definition important), then it's worth paying attention to. And it's worth having open conversations with your employees to ensure that they have their eyes wide open in terms of their performance to your basic expectations. You don't want to be in a situation like the travel company managers were with Brenda.

POINTER

Behavioral expectations are measurable.

Demonstrate Courage to Reinforce Expectations

This final part of step 6 is where the rubber meets the road. Where intention becomes results. Where accountability becomes real. Accountability systems are management tools. Managers hold people accountable. This means that you, as the manager, are responsible for delivering positive and negative consequences for the expectations you've said are required. As I stressed earlier, it is important to deliver both positive and negative consequences, not just negative. If you focus only on punishing deficiencies, your extrinsic motivation system will struggle to work because employees will associate it with pain and suffering, and might not improve performance when you're not looking. (When this occurs, the workplace starts looking and feeling like a parent-child relationship, with the children more motivated to test their parents than do good work.) Here are several examples of ways to reinforce the "gottas":

- **Positive:** Public praise, one-on-one praise, reduced auditing, higher grades/ratings, more discretionary time, milestone badges/notations, bonuses, raises, celebration, promotion or expanded role, perceived perks, incentives, and rewards.
- **Negative:** Additional auditing, lower grades/ratings, withholding rewards, remedial assignments, demotion, removal of perks, counseling discussion, written warning, termination, suspension.

If you've thoughtfully selected the "gottas" and have been open with your team about accountability and your role as their manager, and if you ensure employees know where they stand relative to your basic expectations, then know this: They are expecting you to hold people accountable. They know your job is to help solve performance issues, they hope you'll recognize good performance, and they expect you to do what's warranted. This is how extrinsic motivation systems work and when all parts are clear, it's fair.

This takes courage, always, even for the most seasoned and awesome managers. It's a moment of truth when you decide whether you're going to be open and deliberate and say what might be difficult to say—positive or negative! I've known many managers who seemed incapable of providing positive reinforcement. *Seemed* incapable, but could've done so with a bit more courage (and practice).

Here's an important tip. Reinforcing expectations is easier if you've done the previous parts of this step. When team members know that being a good team member is nonnegotiable, for example, they are not surprised that you hold them to this. A few other thoughts:

- When you call something a "gotta," you are saying it is required. Organizations have requirements. It's OK. This is a professional workplace, not a garage-based startup between buddies. As long as your list of "gottas" is not too long, it'll be fine.

- Some behaviors deserve to be required because they are critical for the success of the organization. I believe that teaming and integrity are at the top of that list and have a low tolerance for actions that run counter to how I've defined these expectations (one more reason why being clear is important—someone's job could be on the line).

- When you hold people accountable, you'll find that fewer people fail to meet your basic expectations over time. Employees will learn and accept the nonnegotiables or leave the organization on their own.

Accountability is an extrinsic, or push, system. And done well, it can enable workplace pull (step 5). Wait, what? Yes, stick with me here. . . . Imagine a team of employees who work well together and do what they say they will. They bring issues and opportunities to each other's attention and support those who need it. They acknowledge and resolve conflict. All of this is normal and expected. The basics are covered for this team and there's little drama or angst getting in the way of their success. Because they have a strong foundation and experience fewer distractions, they can focus on the aspects of their work that provide meaning, challenge, and fun. In other words, they can spend more time with pull.

POINTER

Employees expect you to hold people accountable.

Here's the case for demonstrating the courage needed to hold people accountable. As long as you focus on a few vital "gottas," building a highly accountable team will support your goals for creating a workplace where employees want to do their best work. The extrinsic reward system does not produce intrinsic motivation, but it clears the way—by reducing drama and angst—so that your efforts to create more pull have the space and time to work.

I'm going to repeat a paragraph from the beginning of the chapter, because I think it will have more meaning now that we've explored step 6.

> Accountability is absolutely crucial for organizational success and sanity. And it can be a positive and powerful managerial tool when used with focus and deliberateness. In step six, I'm inviting you to take on a decidedly hopeful view of accountability and how you use it to improve performance and complement your efforts to jack up employee engagement. *Accountability* is not a four-letter word. In fact, it can be a liberating source of organizational peace and prosperity. Really!

Accountability and engagement—push and pull—are both important. And although the managerial practices that increase accountability are not at all similar to what you'll need to do to enhance engagement, these managerial aims are also interdependent. This is a good thing, and it's important to realize as you hone your management craft.

Building ACCEL Skills

The management techniques we've explored in step 6, "Reinforce and Reward the Nonnegotiables," will help you build the following ACCEL skills:

- **Accountability:** Step 6 was all about accountability and helps managers distinguish what they can do to best improve employee accountability where it most matters.
- **Communication:** Every aspect of building accountability requires clear communication with employees—first to establish their understanding of expectations, followed by

sharing feedback about their performance to the standards. As managers practice accountability, they will hone their ability to be clear and specific.

- **Listening and assessing:** To measure performance to expectations, it is critical that managers listen well and assess the meaning of their observations.

Your Turn

Here are a few ways you can practice building accountability:

- Review my list of "gottas" in Example 6-1 and create your own. Share it with your manager and a couple trusted peers to get their input. Try to make your list as short as possible while still acknowledging what's most important.
- Get prepared. Turn up your powers of observation with your list of the "gottas" in mind. Notice how team members act and react throughout the day. Take notes about the current state of performance and compliance and think through how you'll address these before communicating the list to your employees.
- Seek mentoring from another manager you admire for their ability to create a highly accountable workplace that is also open and positive (in other words, don't ask a universally hated manager for advice; select a mentor who has cultivated both push and pull motivation).

The Next Step

In this step, we focused on improving accountability, a necessary part of your managerial regimen. Step 7 will help you bring out the best in others.

Step 7
Bring Out the Best in Others

Overview

- Create connections.
- Enliven minds.
- Cultivate productive irreverence.
- Reinforce collaboration.

This is the ultimate aim, right? Is the reason you are a manager to bring out the best in others? What a cool thing to do for a living. In fact, try using this as your tagline when people ask what you do for a living. Instead of saying you're a middle manager (most of us are in the middle, a terrific place to be, but we all know that saying "I'm a middle manager" tanks any conversation), declare that you bring out the best in others. Talk about a conversation starter! And what a great pull-oriented way of viewing our work.

Saying this is what we do is one thing, but it's another matter entirely to try doing it—actually bringing . . . out . . . the best . . . in others. Quite a heavy thought, isn't it? The good news is that if you define and model excellence (step 3), use pull versus push motivation (step 5), and reinforce and reward the nonnegotiables (step 6), you will create a strong foundation for building great teams whose members do their best work together.

Let's pause a moment to define what I mean by *great team*. I've had managers tell me they loved their teams because their teams gave them no problems. Others look for team members who won't buck the system. Some indicators of team success value when members stick to themselves and focus on their own jobs versus others. OK. To some degree these are all nice behaviors, but a team is a group of people who can accomplish more than the sum of their individual efforts. This is where "best" in *bring out the best in others* lives. And even if your employees do not operate as a team, you should help them maximize the strength of their workplace partnerships and interdependencies. How does this happen? Well, it happens when we appreciate nice behaviors but transcend them to add some edgier ones.

I want employees who will not hesitate to challenge one another or me. I want productive conflict because that's how we grow and learn. I want my team to be a pain in the neck sometimes—business is a contact sport. I want spunk, passion, sharpness, and occasional anger. That's what a great and energized department looks like to me, and I think you could benefit from that kind of team too.

Before you send me a bunch of angry emails, let me remind you that I like niceness. And there's a time and place for peace and harmony and dividing and conquering. I want people to enjoy working together and to help one another out, but that's not the only thing I'm looking for in my team.

As managers, we create the work environment and foster the conditions for the kind of work the team engages in together. Our daily actions, how we structure meetings, how we respond to diversity, our staffing choices, and the questions we ask all communicate the team behaviors we're seeking. If we embrace and reinforce compliance, we'll get lots of it. If we show sincere gratitude when people are candid about concerns, we'll get more candor from everyone on the team. When we promote the productive troublemaker, we send a big message to everyone on the team that it's OK to express real feelings and beliefs.

POINTER

As managers, we create the work environment and foster the conditions for the kind of work the team engages in together.

Create Connections

Business is a contact sport, and management is a social act. Until the robots take over, we need to get things done through people. What that really means is that our relationships are the conduits for results. We explored this theme relative to your success in step 2, "Work Well With Others." Think of a complicated telephone switch box with wires running to each home and then to the telephone company. There are wires of different colors, some with stripes; some are hot, some ground the current. Wires everywhere making each conversation happen. If one wire gets kinked, cut, or corroded, every conversation stops. Your department or team is like that box, and making sure you have each relationship wired and maintained is critical to ensuring the right conversations can occur.

Team members who know each other work better together. They care about each other's successes and are more likely to put up a big stink if things aren't going well. That's what we want—we want people to look out for one another and bring potential problems to the fore. Tolerance, trust, respect, collaboration, and even anger, challenge, and confrontation come from knowing. We need to make sure employees get to know one another, even if they are located in different countries or speak different languages. With the communication options we have available today, there's no reason a team of peers can't develop deep and productive work relationships.

To create the connection is basic—people need to spend time getting to know one another. I'm not advocating a bunch of sit-in-a-corner-chanting team-building sessions or outdoor ropes classes or off-site golf outings. Those get-togethers are OK, but not necessary. I do like facilitated behavioral-style team sessions—like using the MBTI (Myers-Briggs Type Indicator)—but otherwise recommend that you get to know one another by talking about the business. The business is what binds you together. If people have robust and open conversations about the business during their team meetings and morning huddles, you'll find that they'll also have more informal conversations during other times. If you pepper in a few informal team conversations and bring in fruit, granola bars, and vanilla lattes, you'll find that people begin to connect—the carbs and caffeine help and are fun.

POINTER

Tolerance, trust, respect, collaboration, and even anger, challenge, and confrontation come from knowing.

Be careful about the signals you send your team members because our efforts can sometimes cause an unintended reaction. For example, coddling people who have clashes of personality is a well-intended act that ends up hurting relationships. Variety adds spice, and I hope that you have a team filled with people so different they might not want to go bowling together. That said, I've seen very dissimilar people enjoy a game of bowling. Business is business, and we don't have the luxury of working only with those people toward whom we naturally gravitate. In fact, that would be bad for business.

As a manager, you should model productive work relationships with all types of people (step 2) and not tolerate immaturity from others. That's right, immaturity. When professionals use diverse personalities or clashes in style to justify poor partnership, they're being immature. We all have a job to do, and we might need to partner with someone distasteful to us—so what? Get over it and do great work!

People rise to our expectations, so expect that all employees will develop and maintain deep work relationships (step 6). Structure your day and week to reinforce and model this goal. Here are a few examples of how to create workplace connections:

- Begin holding morning huddles for five to 10 minutes so everyone can check in. Over time, huddling will strengthen mutual trust and understanding.
- Help individual contributors learn how their work affects upstream and downstream partners and teams. Encourage interdepartmental relationship building.

- If you have a company lunchroom, make it a point to eat there most days, sitting with peers and employees. Create a positive group conversation.
- Talk about the importance of building deep work relationships and begin every team meeting with business-related questions that prompt each person to share something about their experience, opinions, or ideas.
- Hold more group brainstorming sessions.
- Assign some tasks to pairs and trios. Switch up the pairings you assign so employees get to know their co-workers.
- Ask the training department to facilitate a session about behavioral styles. There are many easy and inexpensive assessments you can use for this purpose, like the MBTI, the DiSC Profile, the Social Style Model, or Activity Vector Analysis.
- Increase the likelihood that team members will converse by changing up their assignments, physical locations, meetings, and schedules.
- A team that feels connected by a common goal or mission will relate more deeply. Make sure that your team members know why they're here and why they're here together. If your employees do not regularly work together, use departmental and company goals as their shared mission.

Creating relationships takes time, so don't be cheap when it comes to ensuring your team spends time together. Sure, each individual has a specific job to do, but each person's success depends on how well individual efforts come together. Great managers are relationship builders because they know that connection forms the foundation that enables best efforts.

POINTER

Great managers are relationship builders because they know that connection forms the foundation that enables best efforts.

Enliven Minds

What's the purpose for a team? Why is a team structure of any advantage? Why don't we just have individual contributors who do their own things? The only reason to have a team and to develop a team is to benefit from the members' abilities to think and work together, strengthen interest and commitment, and thereby make the organization stronger and more successful. That's it; that's why we have teams.

As people managers, it's our job to ensure employees do great work together. Teamwork is a social act, just like management is a social act. The work of teams occurs in conversation—all that teams can do is think, collaborate, decide, and coordinate or plan. And it all starts with good thinking by enlivened minds. I addressed this briefly in step 5, but let's apply the ideas of creating more pull specifically to helping teams do their best work together in the service of organizational goals (*enliven* is an intrinsically driven aim).

I can't count the times that I've seen intelligent and hardworking people performing far below their potential. I'd bet you've seen this, too. Sometimes it's a problem of burnout or maybe the person is in the wrong job. Most of the time, however, it's a management problem. The degree to which our team members' minds are engaged in their work is a direct reflection of our management effectiveness. In other words, it's our fault either way. Individuals might get into a funk every now and then—that's normal. But if we have people on our team who are just going through the motions, we likely have a systemic management challenge.

POINTER

Enlivening minds has a lot to do with making the workplace and the work more fascinating and meaningful.

This—that it's our fault—is a good thing. It also means that we influence what's going well and whether team members engage fully. Notice I wrote *influence*, not *determine*, because we're in the world of pull, not push. I shared a few ideas for increasing engagement in step 5, and Tool 7-1 offers a few specific ideas for enlivening team member minds.

TOOL 7-1
WAYS TO ENLIVEN MINDS AT WORK

Focus Area	Enlivening Technique
Connection to the company	Be as transparent with company information as you possibly can. Keep your team informed. Share their feedback with peers and your manager so they know their voices have been heard.
Energy	Have quick and energetic huddles instead of meetings. Be energetic yourself. Encourage people to get up and move around throughout the day. Hire high-energy people. Help team members manage stress and make sure no one is working too many hours on a consistent basis.
Participation in team conversations	Ask provocative and evocative questions. Elicit everyone's input and show your gratitude for ideas, even contrary ones. Ask people to comment on topics that you know interest them. Send out questions before meetings so people can prepare their thoughts.
New ideas	Share blog posts or articles that highlight trends and innovations in the department's area of focus. Open meetings with short video clips from thought leaders. Ask team members to share articles and videos they'd like to see discussed as a team. Ask team members to see situations and generate ideas from various points of view.
Collaboration	Ask for team or subteam recommendations. Put people into pairs or small groups to work on projects. Acknowledge and reinforce group accomplishment.

STEP 7

Enlivening minds has a lot to do with making the work more fascinating and meaningful. This can be done in any industry or department. Why is your function crucial to the success of the organization? How is it changing? What might new trends offer your department in terms of productivity, efficiency, or service? Ask each team member to tell you the coolest thing they do each day. These questions and others can help your team members fall back in love with their work.

I hate to keep throwing this back on managers, but enlivening minds begins with role modeling. Is your mind alive and engaged? If not, you need to fix that right now because no one wants to get excited about working for an uninspired manager (re-read steps 1 and 2 for some ideas).

Cultivate Productive Irreverence

When we're irreverent, we show a lack of respect for people or things. Productive irreverence, however, is showing a lack of respect for things, processes, practices, and tasks that ought to change so the team can make progress. I'm not advocating that team members demonstrate a lack of respect for one another, but I am encouraging a lack of respect for projects that no longer make sense. Productive irreverence is needed to ensure that you and your team members are questioning practices and tasks that ought to be questioned. Someone who is productively irreverent is an occasional troublemaker and a person you want on your team—more than one would be even better.

Another aspect of being productively irreverent is knowing when and how to communicate concerns and knowing when to keep concerns to yourself. I love occasional troublemakers, I really do. That said, too much is too much! Productive irreverence is selective. I've coached several less-than-selective troublemakers about how to pick their battles for maximum influence and impact.

As the manager, how do you cultivate productive irreverence? Here are two powerful strategies. I bet you can guess the first one—model productive irreverence yourself. Make sure that you challenge the status quo when challenge is warranted and show impatience with continuing to do the wrong things. Managers have told me that their work environment doesn't tolerate productive irreverence. I wonder why that is? Of the people who say this, a small number are stuck—they work for the top-paying employer, need the work to feed their kids, or work in an environment where compliance matters more than contribution. Honestly, this book is written for people who can cultivate influence and improve the workplace culture—or can work toward that end. And I believe that most managers would improve their reputation, not harm it, by being productively irreverent.

Here's a bonus: Being productively irreverent is so much fun! It's fun because breakthroughs can occur when we help our managers, peers, or team members see something in a new way. Breakthroughs are cool. Think about your current list of projects. I bet one or more of those projects ought to be changed or killed. What a relief it would be for the team and business if you crossed irrelevant projects off their lists of worries. And that relates to enlivening the mind as well, because working on a stupid project feels stupid—and draining—and it's no fun.

Here's how you become productively irreverent. Ask yourself if there are tasks, projects, or processes that are taking up people's time and energy but not directly supporting the results you're being asked to produce. Evaluate everything, even small things like reports, meetings, approvals required, or documentation. In some productive way each day, question one action or task with the appropriate people. Here's an example of how you might tee-up that conversation:

> We all have way too much on our to-do lists, and I want to do my part in helping us reduce activities that might no longer make sense relative to our other priorities. I did a quick map of the process we use to get product specifications to the marketing department. Everyone's frustrated with how long this takes, and it's nobody's fault. The process is just very long, and I think there might be a couple places where we can cut steps and make everyone happier.

I call someone who is productively irreverent a prodIR (sounds like "prodder"). Effective prodIRs share their intent first—always something along the lines of making everyone's work life easier and more productive. ProdIRs are a bit like beauty pageant contestants: They always want to create world peace. Productive irreverence is all about making the work planet a lot better. The power of this effort is that when we improve our workplace, everyone raises their game.

STEP **7**

That's how you become a prodIR—start small and start having well-intended, open, and positive conversations that ask, "Why?" But don't get upset if people defend the status quo and decide they want to keep things as they are. Do your best job of explaining the potential opportunities for improvement, and keep plugging away (remember, you still need to be selective to some extent).

Never go negative—that's not productive; it's just plain irreverent. I had a manager friend who'd occasionally blow a gasket if he didn't get his way when he brought up things he thought needed to change. Such immaturity hurt his ability to influence peers and managers and got in the way of his career. Eventually, he overcame this derailing factor—and that was great because had he not changed, he would have become more of a troublemaker than the business could tolerate.

The second strategy for cultivating productive irreverence is to ask for it. Seek all kinds of input and show you're thankful for challenging questions, concerns, and diverse ideas. Call it productive irreverence and ask for it by name when you meet with your team. This will help some members get over the fear of sharing their concerns. Ask for ideas that might seem crazy or impossible. Make it a routine to ask your team members for the tasks on their list that they think aren't worth the effort. Show gratitude, no matter which tasks they identify. Ask clarifying questions to better understand why the task is of low value. Hire people you know will challenge you. Promote employees who take the initiative to try to improve processes and practices, even when doing so might involve bringing up a sensitive topic (like your pet project). If an employee questions your pet project—great! Really, it's great because if it's your pet project, it's important to you and therefore important to do well.

Use Worksheet 7-1 to help your team members think of prodIR ideas. Email everyone the worksheet ahead of the meeting and then ask subgroups of three to five team members to pool their thoughts and present their best collective ideas to the whole team and you. Be thankful for whatever you get, even if their ideas are a bit safe. If you repeat this process regularly, the responses will get better and better. Team members need to learn how to be productively irreverent.

WORKSHEET 7-1
PRODUCTIVELY IRREVERENT IDEA GENERATOR

Category	My Brainstorm Ideas (even wild or "out there" ideas are welcome)
Tasks I'm doing that don't seem to be worth the effort or cost	
Tasks I see others doing that don't seem to be worth the effort or cost	
Tasks my manager is doing that don't seem worth the effort or costs	
Projects or tasks that seem to be misunderstood	
Process improvements that might be unpopular but highly beneficial (e.g., improve quality, output, efficiency, service)	
Work tasks that cause frustration or stress	
Barriers that most get in my way of doing my best work	
Things I could do to better help other team members or teams	

Reinforce Collaboration

Collaboration is a great way to bring out the best in others. This brand of co-creation can be surprising, electric, and highly innovative. What's not to love, right? Most managers will say they want collaboration, but few act consistently with those words. When we set goals, are they individual or team goals? When you fill out a performance evaluation, are you rating individual or team performance? What're the criteria for promotions, pay raises, and bonuses—individual accomplishments or team accomplishments? I'm not suggesting that acknowledging and reinforcing individual excellence isn't a good thing—you should reinforce it. But it's important to notice the balance of what you're

POINTER

Collaboration is a great way to bring out the best in others.

reinforcing so you can determine to what degree your actions and words match your intentions.

People collaborate more when they're given the time, when it's easy to communicate with peers and team members, when they've had the opportunity or practice at working with others, and when they gain a feeling of satisfaction and accomplishment from working together. How many of those conditions exist in your work environment? You can help create the place for all those conditions.

I was talking to a team manager for a software company. He'd done a research project that looked at the effectiveness of project teams. His research showed that the teams who collaborated outperformed the teams who didn't by a longshot. Collaborating teams were several times more productive and successful than their noncollaborating peers. Remember, our goal is to bring out the best in others. This team manager advocates for seating teams together when possible—like in a square of cubicles facing inward with a team meeting table in the middle. This may not be possible or practical in your workplace, but it's good to look at how easy or difficult it is for teams to communicate. Personally, I like letting the team get involved with how their workplace should be arranged.

When I was at Black & Decker (B&D), I was part of an international cross-functional product development initiative where many of the product development team members never saw each other. That made it difficult to encourage collaboration and effective communication. B&D wanted to improve and shorten the product development life cycle, so it got all the global teams together for a four-day training program. One of the best outcomes of that training initiative was that teams met and were able to build relationships and agree on the best ways to communicate and collaborate. They became more interested in one another and committed to their collective success. B&D was very successful in improving its development process, and its next large

POINTER

Your team will perform better when they collaborate. Make sure your actions and words encourage effective collaboration.

new line of power tools—the DeWalt line—was a huge success for the company. Collaboration and communication were key to that success; they will be key to yours, too. Tool 7-2 offers several ways you can reinforce collaboration.

Tool 7-2
Ways to Produce and Reinforce Collaboration

Factor	Ideas for Producing and Reinforcing Collaboration
Physical location	House teams together or in a way that encourages informal conversation. Make sure that informal meeting spaces are available. If the team is located in more than one place, get members together on a regular basis and encourage them to use technology to have both informal and planned conversations. Give them unrestricted access to phone, email, Internet phone, teleconferencing services, and Web seminar software.
Communication processes	Make it a habit to use a portion of your team meetings for collaboration. When people come to your office with questions or ideas, encourage them to gather a few peers to talk through the issue (eventually, they'll do this before coming to you—a beautiful thing).
Tasks and assignments	Assign projects and tasks to teams, subteams, and pairs of peers. Get your team in the habit of working together.
Goals and measurements	Make sure that at least half of your employees' goals are team, subteam, or pair goals. Use team measures along with individual measures for any evaluations, pay raise considerations, promotions, and bonuses. (I don't recommend linking evaluations to pay raises.)
Workplace culture	Reinforce and show appreciation for collaborative work. Model collaboration by asking team members and peers to work with you on your tasks and projects. Encourage diverse opinions and points of view. Show support when team members get together for informal conversations or meetings.

STEP 7

Add these ideas to those offered to enliven minds in Tool 7-1. In particular, I like handing out provocative articles or blog posts to get people talking. Once they get into conversation, team members will transition more naturally into collaborating on specific business issues or opportunities.

This step, "Bring Out the Best in Others," has focused on the team because that's where "best" lives. Whether introvert or extrovert, experienced or newer to the job, it's when engaged employees get together with open, curious minds that their finest efforts emerge and become useful.

Building ACCEL Skills

The management techniques we've explored in step 7 will help you build the following ACCEL skills:

- **Collaboration:** This step will help managers use daily practices that facilitate, enable, and catalyze collaboration.
- **Engagement:** The four parts of this step—create connections, enliven minds, cultivate productive irreverence, and reinforce collaboration—are also managerial practices that will improve engagement.
- **Listening and assessing:** For managers to bring out the best in others, they will need to listen well and assess as a regular part of their managerial regimens. As they practice the techniques offered in this chapter, they will spend more time listening and responding based on the meaning they derive from their team members' contributions.

Your Turn

To bring out the best in others, start by shoring up the practices found in steps 3, 5, and 6. Once you've created this foundation for best efforts, try the following:

- Do a quick assessment of the team elements presented in this step: How strong are the relationships among team members (and with you)? Are your people's minds actively engaged?

Do you have an environment of productive irreverence? Are you productively irreverent? Do team members regularly collaborate?

- Based on your assessment, go back to any section in the step that seems to need improvement and try a few of the techniques I recommend. All the techniques produce a common outcome—they facilitate people spending quality time together and creating better business conversations.
- Embrace your role as a catalytic conversationalist and make every meeting and discussion a great one.

The Next Step

Step 7 has offered you ways to tap into your potential and amp up team outcomes by helping ensure that your team's efforts are focused on the tasks and work that will make the greatest contribution to the organization's goals. Now you are ready for step 8, where I offer my thoughts on the importance of planning.

STEP **7**

Step 8

Plan, Measure, and Adjust

Overview

- Build a habit of planning.
- Share your plans.
- Encourage your team to plan.
- Monitor progress to plans and goals.
- Act with perseverance and agility.

We explored how managers should define their most important priorities in step 1 (know your business) and ways they can translate this into a definition of excellence for their team members in step 3 (define and model excellence). These steps will enable you and your employees to better focus on the work that matters and makes the greatest contribution to the organization. But things change. Circumstances change. New challenges pop up and new opportunities emerge. To ensure alignment and maximize your impact, you'll need to develop strong yet flexible planning practices.

Planning is critical, but it's a relatively rare activity, especially for busy middle managers. We can be more focused and successful if we spend just a few minutes planning each day and week. Most of the managers I've observed don't plan enough. They perceive it as not being fun, something "higher-ups" do, and—most important—

POINTER

Planning helps you make better choices about how to spend your precious time.

not urgent. By definition, planning isn't something that has to be done right now. That makes it a perfect target for procrastination. Of course, we all know that choosing to wait or skipping it entirely will only bite us later because today's urgent tasks probably are looming because we didn't plan in the past. It's a vicious circle—a time-sucking ride you can exit only by developing a regular planning regimen.

Before I share my thoughts on how to plan, I'd like to define what I mean by planning. Some people think they've planned if they've drafted a to-do list—and I guess that is planning at its lowest stage of efficacy. But you're not reading this book because you want to struggle along at a low level of productivity, are you? You're using this book to help you blow the lid off your productivity and success. In other words—simply creating a to-do list isn't good enough to count as your daily planning.

Planning is the combined efforts of thinking about the contributions that you and your team can make today (this week, this month, this year, five years from now) and making specific choices about those actions that will best support your intentions. When you plan, keep both short-term and long-term goals in mind. To achieve long-term goals, work on them a bit each day along with your shorter-term objectives.

Planning isn't boring and mundane—it's where managerial magic happens because it's where you make the decisions about how to spend your time and how to focus your team's energies, passions, and strengths. It's like going on a shopping spree with $5,000 in your hands—choosing what to buy is fun, but it's also important you choose wisely! Your time and your team's time are the $5,000 (and a lot more than that).

STEP

8

Build a Habit of Planning

How will you spend your $5,000? Will you blow it on short-term needs and wants, or invest in the future? Effective planning helps you and your team make the most of your impact on today's and tomorrow's results. To improve your planning practice, develop weekly and daily planning habits.

Weekly Habits

Let's look at some habits you can develop to further your weekly planning efforts:

- Take 30 minutes each Friday afternoon or Monday morning to plan for the upcoming week (adjust the timing if you work a different schedule). Think again about the grand-slam home run described in steps 1 and 3. What would represent a grand-slam home run performance for the coming week (again, thinking about your short-term and long-term goals)? If you and your team excelled, what would occur? Ask your team for thoughts on this in a quick planning huddle (five to 10 minutes).

POINTER

If you do just a little planning on a daily and weekly basis, you will significantly improve focus and results.

- Schedule meetings and conversations that will help you move things forward. Don't just write down, "Talk with Joe about the ABC project timeline"; schedule a meeting with Joe.
- Create a list of decisions you want to make, request, or facilitate, and a list of barriers that need to be obliterated (such as the situations or people that are slowing or pausing progress for you or your employees). Post the list where you'll refer to it daily.
- Think about coaching you can offer that would be most helpful to the team. Identify at least one skill or situation for coaching.

STEP **8**

Daily Habits

Now let's look at some habits you can develop to further your daily planning efforts:

- Spend 10 minutes planning at the beginning of each workday.
- Choose one or two actions you can take today that will make the greatest difference to your short-term and long-term goals. Act on them.
- Take a few minutes to consider each team member's focus for the day. Is each person working on the most important projects or tasks? What adjustments should you make? What support or coaching would be most helpful? Is anyone up against a barrier you can obliterate so they can move forward?
- Take time at the beginning of each day to plan your meeting participation or leadership. Think about the value of the time each person spends sitting around the meeting room table. Meetings are expensive! When people come to meetings unprepared, they waste time and money. Set the standard and ensure your meetings are productive and move work forward.

Your new weekly planning habits will become the foundation for your daily planning. Trust me on this—the process works. Try the weekly and daily planning habits for one month. You'll feel on top of your work and you'll be getting much more accomplished. Worksheets 8-1 and 8-2 offer easy-to-use checklists to make these practices habitual and permanent parts of your managerial regimen. Give these worksheets a try for a month to feel more in control and on top of your busy days.

It feels great to go home after a long day and feel like you actually accomplished something. Without effective planning, you'll be more likely to get sucked into issues and diversions that you regret later.

WORKSHEET 8-1
WEEKLY PLANNING WORKSHEET

Use this worksheet to set aside time and energy for the most important work tasks. Start by defining a grand-slam home run goal for the week. Then write down two to four items for the other planning elements and then use this information to plan your week. Review and revise this worksheet daily or as needed.

Grand-Slam Home Run Goal: _____

Planning Element	My Plan for the Week
Meetings and conversations I need to schedule	
Decisions needed, and by whom	
Coaching and developing, and for whom	
Any must-not-miss items	
Potential barriers to hitting the grand slam	

WORKSHEET 8-2
DAILY PLANNING WORKSHEET

Transfer your weekly grand-slam home run goal from the weekly planning worksheet. Each morning, take 10 minutes to define the actions you intend to take for each planning element. Carry this worksheet with and review it midday to ensure you're on track and focused on the right work.

Grand-Slam Home Run Goal: _____

Planning Element	My Plan for the Day
Two or three actions I can take today that will make the greatest difference	
Team focus—any adjustments to be made	
Barriers I need to obliterate	
Meetings and preparation needed	

Share Your Plans

If you do the weekly and daily planning and then follow your plans, you'll be more productive—I guarantee it. Even if you only follow your plans half the time, you'll still be better off than if you never took the time to plan in the first place. And if you share your plans and planning regimens in ways that inspire (read: create pull) team members and peers, your positive impact will reverberate and expand.

This starts with communicating your plans, but let's be real about plans and planning. Many people would not consider planning to be a fascinating topic. If you schedule a huddle with the subject line "Review of the Weekly Plan," people might come to your meeting, but will team members be eager to hear what you have to say? Language is important; so, communicate in ways that engage and enroll. Here are a few ideas for communicating your weekly or daily plans:

- Show your enthusiasm when you communicate the plan. Focus and alignment are beautiful things!
- Discuss in terms of "setting the week up for success" or "ensuring we spend precious time wisely" or "elements for a great week or day."
- Seek and consider input. Make sure your team members know their participation matters and makes a difference. The phrases "that's just the way it is" or "we're doing it because I said so" should not be in your vocabulary. Some tasks probably will be required, but in those cases be willing to share context to improve understanding and acceptance.
- Thank team members for their time and invite them to offer feedback and updates anytime.
- Keep it simple and brief. Offer clarification and details as needed, but if you communicate plans regularly (at least weekly), employees will become familiar and comfortable with most of the items you list.

Sharing your work plan helps improve clarity and commitment. People will understand what's most important, as well as your focus for the day and week. Block off planning time on your calendar so that employees can see and know that this is something important and useful. Refer to planning time in ways that communicate the value you place on it.

Take the initiative to be inclusive and open. Share your weekly plans with your manager and peers with whom you work closely. This is important and helpful for two reasons. First, if your plan is off target, you want to know! Help others help you by keeping them in the loop. And when you communicate your plans, you will increase the chances that they reciprocate and share their plans with you. This is a good thing, because the more you know about your manager's and peers' priorities, the better able you'll be to proactively support them. Remember step 2, Work Well With Others?

Encourage Your Team to Plan

I'm not suggesting that you ask your team members to do the same type of planning I've recommended you do (30 minutes weekly, 10 minutes daily). That's not realistic, and it's not needed. As the manager, you'll ensure that the team is focused on the most important work. So what kind of planning should individual team members do?

To answer this question, let's start by acknowledging a few typical challenges that workers face. Like managers, employees often have dangling unfinished tasks or projects. Things they've been meaning to complete or are waiting to address. Many also need to seek input or information from others to complete tasks. Team members, like managers, have things they want to do but have not had time to complete. Things like training, seeking coaching or mentoring, committee work, and more. And it's common—at every level—for employees to allow

STEP 8

daily urgent tasks to take over their time. So, what kind of planning should individual team members do? How about if they:

- Define and keep unfinished tasks top of mind.
- Describe and communicate tasks that need input from others.
- Let other team members know about work that keeps getting moved aside by daily firefighting.
- List one task they'd like to do or get scheduled.

Encourage team members to take five to 10 minutes each day to think through these items. All the better if they communicate their mini-plans with other team members. Why? When Bobby shares that he's been unable to finish a quality report due to daily diversions, he'll be more likely to get support to focus on that from other team members. Sima might offer to respond to operational pages from the manufacturing line. Jack might offer to help with the report. And if Bobby shares that he needs the Team A Manager's data for the report, you can chime in and offer to help him get the information he needs.

Worksheet 8-3 offers a format you can use to share and post planning considerations for each team member. If you use a whiteboard, you can create the checklist form with black tape and easily add and erase daily information. I'd recommend you post your weekly planning worksheet with this one so that the whole team can get a fuller picture of their game plan.

You can adjust the team member planning worksheet based on the size and location of your team members and the type of work you do, but you get the idea. Although the type of planning you do, as manager, is different than what your team members will do, having everyone plot out their days with more forethought and consideration is a very good thing for productivity and engagement.

Really? Engagement? Some of you may be thinking that all this planning sounds a bit like micromanagement. Daily planning and daily huddles shouldn't look or feel like that. In fact, when done well, these habits encourage ownership and independence among members of the team. Why do so many managers micromanage? Because they don't have effective communication practices, and they feel uncomfortable not knowing what's going on within the team. Huddling builds awareness and a shared understanding of priorities, but it's never long enough to become a device for micromanagement.

WORKSHEET 8-3
TEAM MEMBER KEY OPEN ITEMS

> Write the names of your team members in the worksheet's left-hand column. Ask each person to share their top two priorities for the day at a morning huddle or informal check-in. Write the priorities in the right-hand column. Refer to this list during meetings and informal conversations throughout the day.

Team Member	Important Open Items and Daily Focus
Bobby	Finish quality report.
Sima	Respond to operational pages from the manufacturing line.
Jack	Create graphs for quality report.
Manager (You)	Schedule short meeting with Bobby and the Team A Manager.
Team Member	
Team Member	
Team Member	

Another potential objection you may have is that holding morning huddles gives the manager too much information from which to micromanage later in the day. If you're a micromanager (offering more direction and control than is warranted to maximize productivity), the information offered in a huddle may be grist for your mill. Here's the simple solution—just don't grind it that way.

I believe the huddle offers managers a good look at what the team is focusing on and which tasks will be accomplished each day. If a team member isn't working on the right things, it's a great opportunity for you to help get their work on track. We

POINTER

Good planning habits encourage ownership and independence among members of the team.

all want our efforts to be focused and worthwhile, so this kind of refocusing should be welcome—not seen as picayune meddling.

I'm a big fan of the team huddle for communicating the weekly and daily focus. I don't like to create a bunch of meetings where people take too much time to go around and say what they're doing. That's often a waste of time. The huddle, on the other hand, is a short, focused, stand-up meeting that accomplishes a lot in a little time. Don't sit—it will lengthen the huddle. If everyone knows they'll huddle for 10 minutes at 9:30 each morning and that each person is expected to share the plan for the day, individual plans will be made before 9:30. This practice promotes good planning. Even those who work on longer term projects have weekly and daily work plans they can and should share.

Monitor Progress to Plans and Goals

Daily and weekly plans support grand-slam goals and your basic expectations. Defining priorities and intentions is important, but the reason we do this work is to maximize the positive impact that our team and function has in the service of organizational strategies. We need to know if things are working, if our efforts are leading to throughput, and if our service is meeting the needs of internal and external customers.

It's tough to address measurements in a book like this because you'll each have unique circumstances. Some of you work in manufacturing environments with well-defined dashboards and quantitative metrics available with a few keystrokes. Others work in disciplines with fewer obvious ways to measure progress. Here are a few examples of ways to create measurement practices that are applicable in most situations:

- Involve the entire team in selecting and measuring indicators.
- Measure results on a regular basis—the same every month—so that it becomes a habit.
- Talk about metrics at team meetings—don't just review them; engage in a meaty conversation about what the metrics are telling you and your team.

- Post the metrics—on common walls, on your office walls, on the intranet.
- Acknowledge and celebrate successes.

Meaningful measurements enable you and your team to discuss your part of the business with some accuracy and specificity. This will lead to richer conversations and better work plans. And as counterintuitive as this may seem, better measures (not micromanagement) will support more workplace pull. Remember that one of the elements that increases pull (step 5) is that the work is worthy of our time and attention. Measurements help team members understand the impact of their work and create a sense of urgency when progress is lacking (another element that creates pull).

When you create measurement practices, you're putting the metrics into your daily and weekly regimens—inviting the data into the department as a respected partner. If you and your team are crystal-clear about the results you need to achieve, have crisp metrics that tell you how you're doing, and have regular discussions about these metrics, your results will improve. We get what we pay attention to.

POINTER

Meaningful measurements enable you and your team to discuss your part of the business with some accuracy and specificity.

Act With Perseverance and Agility

Your weekly and daily planning habits help you and your team steer efforts in the right direction. You've heard the saying, "Plan your work, then work your plan," right? I agree with that wholeheartedly—with one addition. Plan your work and work your plan unless your plan needs to change. To optimize your productivity and impact, be relentless in working your plan while being nimble in case things need to change.

Here's a true story. I presented a plan that had several recommendations to a senior leadership team. I worked hard on the plan and believed in each of my suggestions. The team adopted some of the recommendations and rejected others. The CEO was uncomfortable

STEP 8

with changing certain aspects of the product even though the rest of the team sitting around the table thought the product was getting dusty and needed to change.

After the meeting I was asked if I felt my efforts were wasted because several recommendations weren't adopted. I know there are people who would have answered "yes," but my view is different. I believe that, as managers, we're here to make a difference. It's always our job to prepare and share recommendations about how we think we can improve the business. That said, we have to go where the energy is. To have an impact, we need to get things done. Instead of digging our heels in and becoming stubborn, it's much more effective to move full-steam ahead where we can and make adjustments where we can't. It's more important that we have an impact on the business than that we get there in precisely the ways we planned.

Similarly, it's important not to get too attached to a plan or a project. As I've shared with you a few times earlier in this book, many departments continue to work on projects that should have been killed. Make sure yours is isn't one of those departments. It's good to review plans regularly, and to ask yourself and your team if the items on it still make sense, given the current priorities and what you think they'll be in the future. It feels wonderful—liberating—to kill a project when it ought to be killed. Think of all the time and energy you've saved! You just put your $5,000 back in the bank and made it available for other pursuits.

Note that I'm not addressing yearly planning in this book; however, your daily planning ought to flow from your weekly plans, which should be inspired by yearly or quarterly goals you set as part of the budgeting and planning cycle. I assume that you're working from your departmental business plan or the goals you negotiated with your manager. That said, most of those goals will not be expressed in terms of grand-slam home runs, so you'll want to make those distinctions and additions.

Here's an idea: Share the concept of grand-slam home runs with your peers and manager. They'll love it. They'll thank you. They might even admit that they'd like to "steal" your ideas for planning in this way. Then, you could recommend that you create yearly goals with that level of excellence in mind.

Oh no, are you rolling your eyes at me? OK, start with your area first, and expand after you've had some success using grand-slam goals.

Role modeling agility is important, too. You don't want to cultivate a hair-on-fire work culture, where team members freak out or get stressed every time things change. Be pragmatic, matter-of-fact, and open to changes. Reinforce and show gratitude when team members suggest course corrections or alternative approaches.

Plan the work, work the plan, and make adjustments. Zoom forward!

Building ACCEL Skills

The management techniques we've explored in step 8, "Plan, Measure, and Adjust," will help you build the following ACCEL skills:

- **Accountability:** Building a habit of planning is all about holding yourself and team members accountable for spending time wisely. Becoming proficient in the planning practices shared in this step will improve your accountability skills.
- **Collaboration:** This chapter has emphasized the importance of communicating plans to increase understanding and acceptance.
- **Listening and assessing:** Listening and assessing skills are important for plans to remain relevant and increase team member engagement.

Your Turn

Here are a few ideas for cultivating stronger planning habits:

- Try using the weekly and daily planning worksheets for two weeks. Then modify the practices to fit your style and needs.
- Share your weekly plans with your manager and ask for honest feedback regarding whether you're focusing on the

most important items. Ask for suggestions about regular items to monitor.

- Start asking team members about daily planning considerations. "Sima, do you have anything on your to-do list that we can help you with?" "Rajesa, what's your biggest barrier today?" "I'd like you each to let me know one thing you'd like to learn this week."

The Next Step

This step explored ways to improve weekly and daily planning habits. The next step will help you manage change.

Step 9
Manage Change and Transition

Overview

- Learn how people transition.
- Manage your ability to transition.
- Help others transition.
- Improve departmental agility.

Change is the only constant. You'll face more changes in the next year than you have in the last three years. You read that there is and will be lots of change. You don't need me to tell you about it. However, this does create a management challenge, because many managers struggle to manage change well. This is important because when you and your team members fail to transition, lots of problems get worse. Stack more changes on top of that situation, and the work environment will begin to look and feel very chaotic. This is when people start to burn out and leave. Forget everything regarding pull, because all that goes out the window if employees are too stressed and frazzled to engage.

You should not implement a change without considering the process people go through to transition. Transition is the inner process through which people come to terms with a change. It is the path people have to take to react to and get comfortable with change. The process includes letting go of the way things used to be and growing more at ease with the way things are now. Transition is personal. Each individual will transition at a different speed and in a different way when they're reacting to various changes. In an organization, managing transition means helping people make this process less painful and troublesome. Changes are external; transitions are internal.

Change is very important, but most companies—and most managers—don't invest the time and attention required to ensure that employees transition well. That's a shame because managing transitions isn't rocket science. In fact, when you understand the nature of transition, it's relatively easy to do.

Learning How People Transition

In 1991, William Bridges published an important book, *Managing Transitions: Making the Most of Change,* which addressed how people respond to change. According to Bridges, change and transition are not the same thing. Change is a situation where something transforms: Jobs are added or eliminated, the company merges with a competitor, health benefits decrease or increase, new software is loaded, regulatory requirements increase, or the company reorganizes. Transition is a process of coming to terms with change. To manage a change successfully, managers need to understand and take into account how people transition. Bridges created a transition model describing three phases: ending, the neutral zone, and new beginning, which are outlined in the next sections. Figure 9-1 shows how these phases flow and overlap. There are other models of personal transition, but the Bridges Transition Model is the most comprehensive and has stood the test of time. If you're familiar with my previous books, this is the model I always use and refer to. It's my favorite change management model.

Phase 1: Ending

Every transition begins with an ending, a loss. When things change, employees leave behind the way things used to be. They are left searching for a new way to define their reality. Even if the change is perceived as positive, there is some loss and something that is ending. Before you can transition to the new beginning, you must let go of the way that things used to be.

Sometimes people resist giving up ways and practices that have made them successful in the past. They are reluctant to give up what feels comfortable.

FIGURE 9-1
BRIDGES TRANSITION MODEL

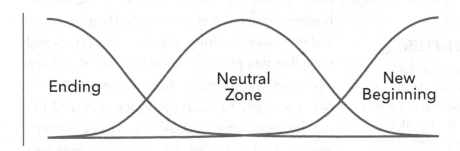

Ending   Neutral Zone   New Beginning

Phase 2: Neutral Zone

The neutral zone is a confusing in-between state, when people are on their way to the new beginning. They are no longer in the past, but not yet to the new beginning, either. It's that ambiguous place in the middle that feels murky. They might feel lost. For some, the neutral zone is so full of confusion that getting through it drains their energies. People are driven to get out of the neutral zone, and some rush ahead while others retreat into the past. But neither of these approaches is advisable because the neutral zone has a purpose.

While the neutral zone can be confusing or even distressing, it also can be a very creative place. Time in the neutral zone is not wasted; this is where the real transformation takes place. The change can continue forward on something close to its own schedule while the transition is being attended to, but if the transition is not dealt with, the change may collapse. People cannot do the things that the new situation requires until they come to grips with what is being asked of them.

STEP 9

POINTER

Time spent in the neutral zone can be very creative. Take time to engage your team in creative new ways to get to the new beginning. There are many paths to the goal.

Phase 3: New Beginning

The new beginning can happen only after people have let go of the past and spent some time in the neutral zone. In this phase, people accept the reality of the change and start to identify with their new situation.

Some people fail to get through the transition because they do not let go of the old ways and make an ending; others fail because they become frightened and confused by the neutral zone and don't stay in it long enough. Some, get through these first two phases of transition, but then freeze when they face the third phase. The new beginning requires people to behave in a new way, and that can be concerning because it tests one's competence and sense of value. Employees will hang back during the final phase of transition if the organization has been known to punish people for mistakes. They will wait to see how others handle the new beginning before jumping in.

POINTER

Situations change, and people transition. Transition is the internal process people go through when they react and adjust to changes.

Tool 9-1 describes possible behaviors that you might see in each transition phase. A person may display one, more than one, or none of the behaviors, but these are the most common.

TOOL 9-1
TYPICAL TRANSITION BEHAVIORS

Transition Phase	Behavior You May See
Phase 1: Ending	Avoidance, clinging to the old, going through the motions, disbelief, shock, anger, mistakes, sabotage, carelessness
Phase 2: Neutral Zone	Detachment, withdrawal, confusion, lack of attentiveness, mood swings, indifference, creativity, risk taking, experimentation, participation
Phase 3: New Beginning	Behavior consistent with the change, focus on purpose, renewed energy, clarity of role, feeling of competence

STEP 9

THE MARATHON EFFECT

Think about a marathon. There are hundreds, perhaps even thousands of people bunched up behind the starting line. The start gun blasts and the folks in the front begin to run. Then slowly the people behind them start to run, and it takes several minutes before the people who were in the back of the line can begin moving. As the race proceeds, the running pack thins out and runners come across the finish line a few at a time over a period of hours.

Transition in organizations is similar. The people planning the change (usually management) start their transition days, weeks, or months ahead of the rest of the organization. By the time the change is rolled out, the managers have crossed the transition finish line (new beginnings), but their co-workers are only starting the transition and won't all run at the same pace. Some will need extra support, and a few may not make it across the finish line at all.

It's important to grasp the marathon effect to understand how people might be feeling so you can show empathy and support for those who are just beginning or are being thrust into endings.

Managing Your Ability to Transition

You've probably seen the safety video on airplane flights—the one in which they tell you, in the event of a loss of cabin pressure, to put your oxygen mask on first before trying to help a child or someone else. I know many parents whose first impulse would be to help their children first. But when it comes to organizational transition, it is important that you put your oxygen mask on first, and then help your team members. You're going to be a lousy leader of change if you're struggling to transition. We can't be stuck and helping others move forward at the same time.

Take a look at the techniques in the next section for helping others. You can apply those same techniques to help yourself transition. Here are some examples:

STEP 9

POINTER

Managers need to ensure they transition well before they can manage change effectively or help others transition.

- Define what's changing for you. What is ending and what are you losing? Mark the ending.
- Make sure you're clear about your part in the transition. Talk to your manager and share your questions and concerns.
- Be patient with yourself; expect that you might have a range of emotions and reactions. This is fine; we all transition in different ways and at differing speeds.
- Set realistic goals for yourself and celebrate successes—even small ones!

If you find that you're struggling with a change, talk to your manager or a trusted peer. Do whatever it takes to make the transition, and then help your team members.

Helping Others Transition

You have a huge opportunity to help your team members, peers, and even your manager (coaching up! help your manager help you and others) transition to changes.

Planning Strategies (Before the Change Is Implemented)

Here are a few strategies to use when planning the transition:
- Talk about transition with your employees. Share the Bridges model so they can help you help others transition and be more aware of their personal reactions.
- Be clear with people about what is ending—from your perspective and their points of view. Identify what they'll lose and how behaviors and attitudes will need to change.
- Plan and schedule communications. Be sure you plan for lots of communication carried on in a variety of ways, including announcement meetings, smaller discussion meetings, daily briefings, handouts, and managing by walking around.
- Learn as much as you can about the change from your manager and peers. Use the structure of the 4 Ps (picture,

purpose, plan, and part) to create a shared understanding that will help everyone leading and involved in the change. What's the picture? What's the purpose? What's the plan? What's my part?

POINTER

To help facilitate acceptance of changes, frequently communicate the 4Ps: What's the picture? What's the purpose? What's the plan? What's my part?

Ending Strategies

Here are a few strategies to use when planning to help your team through the ending phase of transition:

- Communicate, communicate, and communicate. Err on the side of too much communication. Explain the need for the change and why the change makes sense now. Communicate the 4Ps. Define and communicate what is and is not changing.
- Mark the ending. One of the reasons people get stuck in the ending phase is that they don't acknowledge what's ending; they hang on to the old ways. Mark the ending in a respectful and clear way. Openly acknowledge losses.
- Don't be blindsided by people who seem to overreact. Everyone's transition is different, so ensure that you're ready to experience a wide variety of responses.
- Regularly check in with your manager to update them and reinforce what you're doing to mark the ending and help those moving into the fuzzy neutral zone.

STEP **9**

Neutral Zone Strategies

Consider these strategies so you can help team members through the neutral zone:

- Continue to communicate the 4Ps.
- Create temporary systems, roles, policies, and processes to help normalize the neutral zone.
- Set realistic productivity targets; expect some slowdowns.
- Provide training and development to help raise competence and maintain confidence.

- Encourage people to share ideas and participate in refining the details of the change. The neutral zone can be a very creative time, and you want to take advantage of that. Encourage experimentation and idea brainstorming.
- Get people involved in the change plan and working together to make the change seem less isolating.
- Partner with your manager to plan for and agree on temporary practices, roles, and opportunities.

New Beginning Strategies

Here are a few strategies that will help you plan for your team's transition to the new beginning:

- Continue to communicate the 4Ps. Ensure that you communicate often and with consistency. Be open about setbacks and challenges and enlist people to be part of the solution.
- Celebrate successes, even small ones. Reward people for making the transition.
- Ensure that temporary policies and structures are replaced with ones that are consistent with the new situation.
- Reflect on the change and the transitions that people have made. Measure the effectiveness of the change process and identify any outstanding action items.

When in doubt, share the model and communicate the 4Ps! If people don't transition successfully, they can't perform well. Transition is a team competency that, once developed, will serve you and your team through the many changes to come.

Improve Departmental Agility

Helping employees transition well is critical and goes a long way toward ensuring that your team responds well to change. In addition to managing transition, there are things you can do to build team agility and change readiness.

What do I mean by *agility?* Agility is our capacity to be consistently adaptable without having to change. It is the efficiency with which we can respond to nonstop change. Let's break down this definition, because I know it might be a new way to think about change:

- **Consistently adaptable.** When we are consistently adaptable, we can modify how, when, and where something is completed with the same confidence and efficiency that we use to run a routine report. Zigging and zagging is second nature and being adaptable does not cause great stress or worry.

- **Without having to change.** Returning to our definition of agility, what does without having to change mean? What would this look like in action? Imagine a professional tennis player named Bjorn. In between tournaments, Bjorn practices dozens of shots with a variety of practice partners on hard, grass, and clay courts. Each tennis match is unique, but he will be better able to respond to each new challenge because he has trained himself to adapt quickly. As business professionals, we can train in the same way and increase our ability to respond to new situations without having to change our overall approach.

- **Efficient responses.** When individuals resist change, the efficiency with which they can adapt is reduced because a part of their attention and time is spent moving away from the direction of progress. When we do not resist and, in fact, are highly adaptable, we can progress toward our goals faster and with fewer diversions. Resistance creates organizational mental garbage that can build up and contribute to a culture that will be hard to combat or change.

Sounds great, right? And daunting to think about? Well don't worry, building agility is straightforward and can be done during the normal course of your current daily practices. That said, agility is a systems-based capacity, not a singular trait. It takes more than will, or an open mind, to be flexible. Agility will allow team members to

STEP 9

build into everyday practices an ability to nimbly respond to changing circumstances and take advantage of emerging opportunities. When your team is agile, changes do not stress members as much because this is a normal way of working.

What can managers do to build team agility? You can improve nimbleness in three systemic (systemic, as in systems thinking, not computer/IT systems) components including focus, resources, and performance:

- **Focus (direction of the work):** What people are doing. This includes how you define goals and priorities and your planning practices. We've explored these areas quite a bit in this book. The more inclusive and flexible your planning processes, the better they will support team agility.

- **Resources (speed of outputs):** How you spend financial, time, and people assets and whether you have regular mechanisms to reassess and realign your resource allocations. This is not just about how many people you employ or how many hours they each work, but also how you define roles and whether you regularly realign roles and responsibilities. Management of costs and opportunity costs (loss of potential gain when one alternative is chosen over another) also fall into this category.

- **Performance (efficiency of the work):** How success is measured and reinforced, and how capability is created. This element focuses on metrics of all kinds and the formal and informal ways we ensure we know how things are going. If you have a good pulse on current strengths and barriers, you and your team members can comfortably respond and adjust to keep performance humming and on track.

These bullet points might seem more philosophical than practical, but I wanted to explain the concept of agility in a way that might give you ideas for how you can increase agility in your department. Tool 9-2 offers several simple practices that can help.

TOOL 9-2
WAYS TO IMPROVE AGILITY

Systemic Component	Ways to Improve Agility
Focus (direction of the work)	Daily and weekly planning, regular debriefs, reassessments, looking inside and outside for benchmarks, goal setting, productive irreverence
Resources (speed of outputs)	One-on-ones, role assessments and changes, start/stop/continue exercises, seeing things from the internal or external consumers' mindset, budgeting and rebudgeting, opportunity costs analysis
Performance (efficiency of the work)	Process improvement, MBWA (managing by walking around), removing barriers, targeted task teams, analysis, performance metrics, clarifying expectations, accountability, engaging others

Many of the management techniques we've explored in the first eight steps help improve agility. That's by design because as a manager, your job is to bring out the best in others and agility is an enabling factor.

If you help employees transition and "bake in" organizational agility practices, you and your team members will be able and prepared to respond to continuous change and say, *bring it on.*

Building ACCEL Skills

The management techniques we've explored in step 9, "Manage Change and Transition," will help you build the following ACCEL skills:

- **Communication:** Many of the techniques we explored in this step will help you practice effective communication skills that are specific, open, and helpful for enabling transition.
- **Listening and assessing:** Since transition is the process for how we, as humans, react to changes, listening plays a significant role. Managers who practice communicating the

4Ps, for example, will hone their ability to listen fully and assess the meaning of what employees say, even when their concerns are not initially obvious or clear.

Your Turn

Here are a few ways you can build your skills at managing change and transition.

- Use the Bridges Transition Model to help you plan for and manage your next change.
- Share the model with your team and create communication strategies that will help you facilitate transition.
- Talk openly with your team members about the phases of transition and remember that each person may transition differently.
- Read William Bridges's book, *Managing Transitions*. It includes a case study exercise that management teams should do together before implementing any large change initiative.
- Brainstorm ways to improve departmental agility regarding focus, resources, and performance systemic components.

The Next Step

This step helped you learn about agility and how to help employees transition. In the next and final step, you'll tap into your reasons for managing and the ways you can define the legacy you want to leave.

Step 10
Build a Career, Leave a Legacy

Overview

- Visualize your legacy.
- Be what you seek.
- Leave things in better shape.

Management can feel like a thankless, stressful, and difficult profession. Most of us don't do this kind of work for the money or the fame, and we often get neither. We manage because we want to make a big difference. We step up and into workplace dysfunction and muck because we know we can leave things looking, sounding, and feeling better than how we found it. That's the vision that ties millions of us together. I love working with managers because they're the engines of the organization. If the engine starts running 10 percent better, the effect is amazing. The particular shape of that impact is your legacy. When you leave the job or company, what mark do you want to leave behind?

Let's do a little reality check here. How many of you have taken over a new job and found that your predecessor left the department in shambles? Roles are unclear, people are fried, and projects aren't getting done on time. That happens a lot—and not just when a manager is terminated. Why do many talented and smart managers leave a mess for the next person?

Let's think about why people leave jobs. Many of the managers I know who've quit left their jobs when they were burned out and couldn't take it any longer. We rarely leave jobs at the height of our effectiveness, but I'd like to propose that you do. Unless you're about to have a stress-induced heart attack or something else dire, make sure you leave your department looking and feeling great. Instead of short-timer's disease (becoming a lame duck during your last two weeks), try setting a new standard in leaving well. It feels great to go out that way.

Visualize Your Legacy

What kind of a legacy would you like to leave? Is there a particular project for which you want to be known? Would you like to create an amazing team? Do you want to revolutionize the way your company plans for innovation? Do you want to lead record-breaking gains in financial performance? Imagine that you're a fly in the elevator one week after you leave. Two people are talking about you. What would you like them to say?

POINTER

All managers should think about the legacy they wish to leave. Creating a legacy vision will help shape your actions and results today and in the future.

In addition to the broad or grand accomplishments you seek, think about the ways in which you want to be known as a role model. Do you want to be remembered as the queen of exciting meetings? (That would be my goal.) Or the king of provocative analysis? Do you want to be known as always organized and prepared? Creative and innovative? Fun? Think about how you want to be known and the type of reputation you want to build. Write down your rough thoughts in Worksheet 10-1.

Can you visualize your legacy—see it come to fruition? Notice the details of how success looks and include them in your weekly and daily planning regimen (step 8). Spend three to four minutes every morning and afternoon visualizing the legacy you want to leave. Repeated visualization is a powerful tool that will seep into your daily choices, actions, and conversations.

STEP 10

WORKSHEET 10-1
CREATING YOUR LEGACY VISION

Think about the legacy you want to leave for each aspect of management listed in the left-hand column. Then write your legacy goals in the spaces provided in the right-hand column.

Aspects of Management	The Legacy You Want to Leave
Results and contribution to the business	
Team health and development	
Peer partnership and collaboration	
Creativity and innovation	
Processes and practices	
Workplace culture	
Systems and structure	
Change and agility	

Be What You Seek

One of my all-time-favorite quotes is from Mahatma Gandhi: "You must be the change you wish to see in the world." I believe that's true, and I remind myself of it often when I'm dissatisfied with a result.

If you're leaving your legacy today, the question is, are you leaving the legacy you want to leave? If you want to be known for helping turn the department around, start turning it around today. If you want to be known for being prepared and organized, be that today.

Being the change today doesn't mean that we've arrived at the final level of performance; it means that who we are being is consistent with our goals. A really clear way to describe this is to use the example of diet and fitness. Let's say you are 50 pounds overweight and inactive. Your goals are to be vibrant and healthy and, one day, to run a marathon. You can't run a marathon today and you shouldn't try, but you can behave in a way that is consistent with being vibrant, healthy, and a runner:

- **Consistent:** Eat lots of fruits, vegetables, whole grains, and lean protein; walk two miles; do 20 minutes of weight training; finish the evening with 20 minutes of yoga stretching and relaxation.
- **Not consistent:** Say you'll exercise tomorrow; have a cheeseburger, fries, and cola for lunch three days in a row; think about what you'll eat differently tomorrow.

The distinction is pretty clear. Sure, everyone can have a cheeseburger every now and then, but, on balance, are you being the change you seek to make in this world or your company? I once worked alongside and coached a friend who wanted to leave a legacy of a strong and collaborative leadership team. The problem was that his style was sometimes too provocative, pushy, and intense. He was the biggest barrier to the team's collaboration. On days when he remembered that, he was able to be consistent with his goal and to modify his approach to build conversation and collaboration. The best way to ensure that you leave the legacy you seek is to start being it today.

Leave Things in Better Shape

Here's a pet peeve of mine: I start a new job, get into my new office, look around, check out the desk and file cabinets—and there's junk everywhere! Unused ketchup packets in the top right-hand drawer, tons of stuff filling the inbox, and what looks like an open bag of roasted peanuts in the top drawer commingling with 85 half-used pens, 23 bitten-on pencils, and 13 bottles of dried-up White-Out. How many of you have started a new job and had this same experience? How many of you have left offices in this shape? Come on, be honest! Please don't do this to the next person. Leave your workspace in great condition—better than when you got it. I bet some people never bother to clean out the peanuts and end up passing them on to manager after manager after manager, like a Christmas fruitcake.

STEP 10

Show pride in the work you've done and help pave the way for the next person's success. Even if you're leaving because you can't stand the job any longer, take the high road.

POINTER

Show the organization how to leave with style and grace—leave your department and office in better shape than you received it.

My example only went so far as to describe the desk (but it's an excellent visual, no?). You need to do the same with projects, initiatives, personnel challenges, and incomplete tasks. Leave them all in better shape than when you took over the job. I once inherited the job of a woman who did not even take the time to delete her personal emails. Her emails were transferred to me so that I would have the vendor contacts, but I also got lots of creepy messages about her dates and shopping habits. That's just plain lazy and, in these days of enhanced access, dangerous because you never know what's going to end up on some blog or written in a management book as an example of "don't do this." Take the last two weeks to clean things up in general, and have fun going out with a glorious bang.

Start living your legacy today, even though you may not leave this job for years. Improve the team's strength and capacity. Improve processes. Be the fullest expression of your unique self and give your organization the very best you have to offer. Establish a better process for managing new projects. Teach the organization how to have fun and get a lot done.

Building ACCEL Skills

The management techniques we've explored in step 10, "Build a Career, Leave a Legacy," will help you build the following ACCEL skills:

STEP 10

- **Accountability:** To leave a legacy, you'll need to bring your vision to fruition. Managing consistent with your vision is accountability in action. So as you hone your vision and practice acting in alignment with it, you'll be building personal accountability.

- **Collaboration:** To leave a legacy, you'll need to include, learn from, and work with many others. Collaboration is at the heart of making things better.

Your Turn

Here are a few thoughts about how you can practice step 10:

- Do you know the legacy you want to leave as a manager? The time to start thinking about that is now, not six months before you leave the company.
- Things change and you'll change. Take some time to think about the impact you want to have and how you can best act in alignment with that vision today.
- Consider your managerial vision when you do your weekly and daily planning.

Conclusion

There you have it—my 10 steps to better management. Are they the only steps? No. Are they sequential steps? They don't have to be. Are they really steps at all? Who knows—it depends on how you look at them. That being the case, here's something I wholeheartedly believe: If you utilize the techniques suggested here, you'll have a more fruitful and enjoyable career as a manager. I've seen how the best managers do it, and this is what has worked for me.

You might be wondering whether you can do it *all*—all 10 steps. It's a lot to take in, for sure. But I know that you can do it. Maybe not at first, but over time. Management is a craft you hone. The steps work together and complement one another. To help you see how the 10 steps work together, and to assure you that you don't need to "swallow the sun," we've created a fun and helpful visual, which you can find on the next page.

Oh, there's one more step, let's call it step 11. Well, it's not really a step, but it's something important to mention. If you're going to be a manager and you're going to dedicate your career to one of the toughest and most vital jobs there is (remember, you're the engine!), then it's critical that you have fun.

Do you let your job suck you into its vortex of tasks, reports, emails, and stacks of reading material? Having fun and doing great work are complementary—you can and should do both. It's fun to be focused and moving forward; and when we have fun, we have more energy for our work. Fun is different for each person. You don't have to explode in extroverted joy at the sight of the office supply delivery. Just make sure that you enjoy your work and that your pleasure shows. As the manager, you need to model a focus on fun and to encourage your team members to have fun, too. If you honestly don't find your work

10 Steps to Be a Successful Manager

Step 10: Build a Career; Leave a Legacy

Step 9: Manage Change and Transition

Step 8: Plan, Measure, and Adjust

Step 7: Bring Out the Best in Others

Step 6: Reinforce and Reward the Nonnegotiables

Step 5: Use Pull Versus Push Motivation

Step 4: Hire for Fit and Onboard for Success

Step 3: Define and Model Excellence

Step 1: Know Your Business

Step 2: Work Well With Others

to be fun, change your job. Life's too short to toil away at work that gives you no pleasure or satisfaction.

Fun = pleasure. Pleasure is the feeling of happy satisfaction and enjoyment. It comes from being positive, and if you have a positive outlook and express optimism for the future, you'll go a long way toward creating an attractive work environment. And it's infectious! When you infuse the work environment with positive energy and a caring spirit, you set the tone for all the other relationships in your area. Be fun and show optimism. (Are we on step 12?)

And you must also be humble (step 13). If you want to be a successful manager, be authentic and show humility. Perhaps you've seen the opposite rewarded? Power trips, unchecked egos, and a disproportionate reverence for hierarchy used to be tolerated in some organizations. And corporate cultures sometimes rewarded these managers by calling them strong. But! Being an overbearing boss has never been a good thing. Can you be humble and strong? You bet. Be assertive, deliberate, committed, and humble. It's important to distinguish authority driven by position and the strength that comes from commitment and care. When we are humble, we are able to access our strengths and use them for good. Do that.

Relax! (Step 14?) Try not to take things so seriously. I knew a manager who had a big and dramatic reaction to everything. He blew little issues and opportunities way out of proportion. He took his job and the work far too seriously, and he stressed out everyone around him. He could be a likable guy, but he oozed anxiety and nobody wanted to work with him. Unless you're the secretary-general of the United Nations or an emergency room trauma doctor, I'm sure you can relax more.

Management is a customer service job. To provide good service, we need to relax and do unto others (step 15). I bet you think I'm going to write "do unto others as you want others to do unto you." I guess you're right because I just wrote it, but that's not the point I'm making here. My point is simpler: Do unto others. Help people out. Do nice things for people. Be thoughtful. Take the time to be a nice person. When you do your daily planning (step 8), ask yourself what you can do for someone today, and then do it.

It's altruistically selfish to be nice to others! If you're nice and helpful, your peers and employees will come to your aid when you need it most. Imagine you just made a huge mistake and put the progress of a product launch on hold. Imagine that you need an extraordinary effort from everyone on the team to help you turn the situation around and get the product launch back on track. Now imagine you're in this situation and you haven't paid any attention to your team members. You haven't been particularly nice or helpful because you've been so self-absorbed with personal priorities. You're in a bit of trouble. Now picture it differently: You're a beloved manager who always goes out of your way to help others and show care. Your problem is solved.

OK, that's it, that's *all* you have to do to be a great manager.

• • •

People who want to manage—people like you—are amazing, and I have a tremendous amount of respect and admiration for you all. As a trainer, coach, and fellow manager, I'm always interested in learning about the techniques that work best for you. Please consider dropping me an email with your feedback, ideas, and stories. You can find my current email address on my website, www.lisahaneberg.com.

Much success!

References
and Resources

Bridges, W., and S. Bridges. 2017. *Managing Transitions: Making the Most of Change,* 4th ed. Boston: Da Capo Press.

Chermack, T.J. 2011. *Scenario Planning in Organizations: How to Create, Use, and Assess Scenarios.* San Francisco: Berrett-Koehler.

Csikszentmihalyi, M. 2008. *Flow: The Psychology of Optimal Experience.* New York: Harper Perennial Modern Classics.

Friedman, R. 2015. *The Best Place to Work: The Art and Science if Creating an Extraordinary Workplace.* New York: TarcherPerigee Books.

Haneberg, L. 2005. *Organization Development Basics.* Alexandria, VA: ASTD Press.

Haneberg, L. 2012. *The ASTD Management Development Handbook.* Alexandria, VA: ASTD Press.

Mitchell, T.R., B.C. Holtom, T.W. Lee, C.J. Sablynski, and M. Erez. 2001. "Why People Stay: Using Job Embeddedness to Predict Voluntary Turnover." *The Academy of Management Journal* 44(6): 1102-1121.

Napier, R., and E. Sharp. 2018. *Not Just Another Meeting.* Alexandria, VA: ATD Press.

Pink, D. 2011. *Drive: The Surprising Truth About What Motivates Us.* New York: Riverhead Books.

Sanders, T. 2006. *Likeability Factor: How to Boost Your L-Factor and Achieve Your Life's Dreams.* New York, NY: Crown Business.

Sinek, S. 2017. *Leaders Eat Last: Why Some Teams Pull Together and Others Don't.* New York: Portfolio.

About the Author

Lisa Haneberg is an organization development, human resources, leadership, and management author, practitioner, and consultant. She has more than 30 years of experience providing executive and management development and training and coaching solutions for large and small organizations. She has particular expertise in the areas of senior team development, performance management, executive coaching, talent management, succession planning, organizational agility and alignment, and middle management effectiveness.

Lisa's written several books, including *Coaching Training; Coaching Basics*, 2nd Edition; *Developing Great Managers: 20 Power Hours; Double the Love: 11 Secrets for Building Highly Accountable and Engaged Teams; Focus Like a Laser Beam: 10 Ways to Do What Matters Most; Organization Development Basics; Two Weeks to a Breakthrough: How to Zoom Toward Your Goal in 14 Days or Less; The High Impact Middle Manager: Powerful Strategies to Thrive in the Middle;* and *Coaching Up and Down the Generations*. In addition, her work has been highlighted in publications such as *Leader to Leader, Washington CEO, Capital,* and *Leadership Excellence*.

Lisa has held both internal and external consulting roles in organizations such as Memorial Hermann Health System, MedCentral, Black & Decker, Mead Paper, Intel, Amazon.com, Corbis, Promedica, MTD Products, Perfetti vanMelle, TUI Travel International, Aultman Health Care, OPW Fueling Components, Royal Thai Government, the FAA, the EPA, Microsoft, Premera Blue Cross Oregon, and the City of Seattle.

Lisa holds a BS from the University of Maryland and an MFA from Goddard College. To learn more about her work, visit her website at www.lisahaneberg.com.

Index